Forged by the Knife

The Experience of Surgical Residency from the Perspective of a Woman of Color

PATRICIA L. DAWSON, M.D., Ph.D., FACS

Patricia L. Dawson

OPEN HAND
PUBLISHING INC.

OPEN HAND PUBLISHING INC.
Seattle, Washington

OPEN HAND PUBLISHING INC.

P. O. Box 22048, Seattle, Washington 98122-0048
206-323-2187 / 206-323-2188 fax
openhand@jps.net / www.openhand.com

Design and production: Deb Figen, Art & Design Service
206-725-2892 / artdesign@jps.net

Cover illustration and calligraphy: Susan Russell

Library of Congress Cataloging-in-Publication Data

Dawson, Patricia L., 1949-
   Forged by the knife : the experience of surgical residency from
the perspective of a woman of color / Patricia L. Dawson. -- 1st ed.
      p.   cm.
   Includes bibliographical references.
   ISBN 0-940880-63-6 (cloth : alk. paper). -- ISBN 0-940880-64-4
(pbk. : alk. paper)
   1. Afro-American women surgeons Case studies.   2. Surgery--Study
and teaching (Residency)--United States.   3. Afro-American women
surgeons--Training of.   4. Afro-American women surgeons--
professional relationships.   I. Title.
   [DNLM: 1. Internship and Residency--United States Personal
Narratives.   2. Surgery--United States Personal Narratives.
3. Minority Groups--United States Personal Narratives.   4. Women--
United States Personal Narratives.   WZ 100 D2728 1999]
RD28.A1D39   1999
617'.0071'55--dc21
DNLM/DLC
for Library of Congress   99-35331
                                                              CIP

FIRST EDITION

Printed in Canada
02 01 00 99   4   3   2   1

TO EVERY WOMAN
who has struggled and sacrificed
to reach her goal of becoming a surgeon.

Forged by the Knife

We have taken the long and difficult journey,
      alone, isolated, afraid.
We have traveled up the Amazon, braving
      the dangerous jungle full of snares,
      ambushes, and wildlife.
We have been submerged, diving for the gold,
      risking pain and injury.
We have been isolated in boot camp, hiding
      our identities and taking abuse
      from drill sergeants.
We have gathered up our strengths, immersed
      ourselves in our dreams, lived for the
      transcendence, and put our emotions away
      in order to do what we needed to do.
Now we are surfacing and reclaiming ourselves —
      our needs, our lives, our hearts, and souls.
We are peeling the orange of our experiences,
      taking the sting of the juice in the eye
      to reach the sweet fruit at the center.
We take the pain, the fatigue, the isolation,
      and we arise from our trial by fire
      like the phoenix to create a new being.
Forged by the knife,
      we take the meaning
      we create from our experiences
      and we create a new world,
      we create a new way of being; we create
      a new community of Black women surgeons.

Contents

Preface

This book arose from the dissertation I wrote to complete my Ph.D. work at The Fielding Institute in Santa Barbara, where I was fortunate to do my studies. The Fielding doctoral study process encourages flexibility, exploration, detours, and personal growth as essential elements of the learning experience. Possibly my greatest accomplishment in achieving my Ph.D. was learning more about myself and the things that I hold to be important and close to my heart.

A Black woman general surgeon myself, the dominant memories I had about my residency experience were of pain and isolation. Although my training taught me to be an excellent surgeon, it never nurtured my spirit. Instead, it consisted of a series of spirit-crushing episodes. For many years after finishing residency I didn't want to think about it, didn't want to relive either the high points or the low points. But after about ten years had passed, I became interested in understanding that crucial period in my life. So I entered graduate school and chose to study the residency experiences of other Black women general surgeons, hoping they would give me insight into my own experience.

As a Black woman surgeon I have often felt very isolated. I have spent most of my training and professional life in situations where I was the only Black female, and often the only female. My reactions to events have often been very different from the reactions of my colleagues. In these situations I have felt both invisible and hyper-visible. It has been difficult to find allies. Consequently, I have carried with me a (largely unspoken) burden of pain and isolation. Never had I heard a male surgeon speak of the personal trauma of surgery residency, the pain suffered and the sacrifices made to become a surgeon. I knew that these topics couldn't just be "my issues," but they seemed to be unacknowledged or forbidden. In studying other Black women general surgeons, I was opening the door to exploration of my own experiences.

Other physicians' and surgeons' reactions to this work have been varied. I have presented the women's stories and my interpretations at various forums — including the Surgical Section annual luncheon of the National Medical Association, the Black physicians organization; the Stanford University McGann Series for medical students, and at my local hospital. I always have a twinge of discomfort, as if I'm speaking of things that are supposed to remain unsaid. Many of the women have been supportive and relieved to find that others have shared some of their difficulties, have had similar experiences and feelings. Some of the surgeons at the NMA meeting were defensive, reacting as if I were unfairly criticizing their residency programs. Either the topic or the forums did not draw White male surgeons, since there has been only one (self-identified) White male surgeon in any of my audiences. He told me that the experiences I discussed mirrored his own. He was eager to share his own stories of isolation and pain during his residency.

It may be that there are a number of surgeons who are now ready to examine not only the benefits of their residencies but the emotional and psychological prices they paid. It may be that there are increasing numbers of surgeons who have reclaimed the human side of their identity they may have buried during training. It may be that there is now increasing opportunity for surgeons to recognize one another as more whole individuals and to develop a surgical community that fosters sharing, understanding, and healing. I hope this book may help to make that happen.

Acknowledgments

I want to acknowledge two people who were inspirations to me: my father, P. Gordon Dawson, M.D., and his mother, Alma Lucille Thomas. My father's courage, honesty, and resilience have always been a source of strength to me. His desire to be a surgeon was thwarted by circumstance and his life was impacted by racism, but he was an outstanding general practitioner and an on-going role model for me.

Grandmother Alma Lucille Thomas was my model of determination, grace, competence, and caring. A woman of strong opinions and strong faith, she taught me that there is nothing a Black woman cannot do if she puts her courage, strength, and faith behind it.

I want to thank my husband, Stanley; my daughter, Alexandria; my son, Wesley; and my mother, Claire, for their patience, love, and support. I would like to thank my Fielding dissertation committee: the chair, Dr. Argentine Craig; Drs. Miguel Guilarte, Jody Veroff, and Michele Harway; and the student member, Ann Francis. I also want to acknowledge my external reader (a scholar not affiliated with Fielding), Dr. Joycelyn Elders, who provided me with thoughtful feedback.

Editor Phyllis Hatfield and publisher Anna Johnson have made the publishing process pleasurable. Their support and enthusiasm have been highly appreciated.

Most importantly, I thank the participant surgeons, without whose determination, openness, and honesty this book could not have been accomplished. Their stories are the heart and soul of this work.

Chapter 1

Opening the Door to Understanding

Feminist researchers Reid and Kelly have written, "Women of color are frequently scrutinized as helpless recipients or victims of society. Few researchers attempt to examine strengths and survival strategies used by women of color. Fewer studies examine these women as enactors, enablers, or as potential individuals."[1] In 1996 I decided to study just such a group of individuals — Black women general surgeons — and how the experience of residency training influenced their sense of self. I had several purposes in mind. First, I wanted to capture the experience of a significant subgroup and, in so doing, create a space where the voices of an historically silenced population could be heard. Second, I wanted to examine the personal impact of surgical training on this group of women, and thereby gain a new perspective on the formative years of surgical education and socialization. Third, I felt that this research could broaden our understanding of the experience of Black women in nontraditional professions. Lastly, I hoped to contribute to the field of feminist research; by incorporating feminist values in my work, I acknowledged this group of Black women surgeons as co-creators of knowledge and meaning by exploring their experiences and weaving their voices together.

I have been asked frequently why I wanted to earn a Ph.D. and why I wanted to do this research. At the time I started graduate school, I was working as a general surgeon in a large health maintenance organization. A portion of my time was spent as the director of medical staff diversity. In this capacity I needed to understand the significance of patient and physician diversity on health, wellness, and health care delivery. It was my job to help formulate policy and make strategic plans, and to educate others about diversity and clinical cultural competence. I was very much engaged in on-the-job learning and wanted to enrich my learning by being part of an educational community. I believed that if I was going to be doing that much studying, I might as well be receiving academic credit for it. As an African American female, I have found it necessary to prove my self repeatedly to others, and academic degrees can be an important tool in accomplishing this.

One of the most important lessons I learned in the course of this study was that I had to know myself in order to learn, grow, and teach others. My dissertation research — the material presented in this book — gave me an opportunity to uncover and explore, through others' experiences, an experience that had an immense impact on me. I wasn't sure what I would discover when talking with the research participants, and I was surprised at the results, but on reflection, found them to ring very true for me.

I am a Black woman general surgeon who completed medical school in 1977 and then entered a five-year surgical residency. When I started medical school I never imagined that I would want to be a surgeon; my father was a general practice physician, and I assumed that I would go into internal medicine. As a third-year student my first clinical rotation was in internal medicine. The resident physicians on this service all seemed depressed and unhappy. They were working with patients with chronic medical conditions who rarely got better and frequently did not follow their doctors' instructions. My second three months were spent on the surgical services. I started out working with the trauma team in an inner-city hospital. When a patient arrived in the emergency room with a gunshot wound or stab wound we would swoop in, insert IVs and catheters, and whisk them off to surgery. I found the technical aspects of surgery fascinating. Usually the patients recovered from their injuries and went home. The surgeons were all having a great time. They were excited about their work, happy to be there, and enjoying the immediate gratification of seeing their patients get well. From that point on, I knew I wanted to be a surgeon.

There were two women general surgeons on the faculty of my medical school, neither of whom took any particular interest in the women students and residents. My first two years of surgical training were spent in an East Coast program with about 75 residents, only four or five of whom were women, mostly White; a woman from India and I made up the diversity in the women's group. There may have been one or two other Black resident physicians, but we were spread out enough that our paths did not cross very often. In this training program we did a lot of trauma surgery, and I quickly tired of dealing with the violence that was so prevalent. The trauma of auto accidents was one thing, but most often we were treating the victims of gunshot wounds and stabbings. I felt that I was ready to learn more about surgical illness and elective surgical procedures, so for my last three years of training I transferred to a smaller residency program on the West Coast.

Here there were about 15 residents in a five-year general surgery training program. Although it was one of the oldest training programs in the Western United States, only one other woman had finished the program before me, and that had been nearly a decade earlier. During my tenure there were three female interns, none of whom stayed in general surgery. There were no other Black residents in the surgical program or in the other residencies. There were also no Black physicians on staff in that medical center, and for my first two years, no female physicians.

Residency was a difficult and challenging time, placing me in a world that was alien in virtually all respects. As a medical student and intern I had worked with a Black male neurosurgeon who was a role model and support to me, and a female orthopedic surgeon who showed some interest in my career, but the vast majority of surgeons with whom I worked were White males who had little interest in mentoring me and little experience with female surgery residents. During my training I once contacted and talked with a woman general surgeon in the same city, but had no ongoing relationship with her. Several years passed after I completed residency before I even met another Black woman general surgeon.

In my limited contact with them, I had experienced other female surgeons as falling into several general categories: those who are at least as macho as the men, and who remember the tribulations of residency with relish; those who maximize their femininity and minimize the difficulties and sexism encountered during residency; and those who, from some vantage point, find themselves changed and wounded by their residency experiences. The macho women tended to act like many of the male surgeons; they bragged about how many nights they had gone without sleep, they could be crude, and they made callous statements about their patients. Their tough demeanor declared that they were surgeons first and only incidentally female. The second group stressed their femininity by always wearing makeup — even in the middle of the night; they wore heels and dresses, kept their long nails polished, and flirted with the men. They seemed to want to emphasize that they were "real women" as well as surgeons. Surgeons in the third group were much rarer and harder to identify because they rarely spoke of their residency experiences or exposed their pain. I knew that I fell into the third group, but often wondered if I was the only one.

For me these are not static categories, and the first two stereotypical behaviors may well be different coping mechanisms, each of which may be useful or "natural" at different times. But our differences, and the scarcity of women in the third group who seemed to be like me, served to alienate me from many of the women surgeons that I met.

My residency experience was complex. I loved learning surgery and caring for patients, and I had as teachers many excellent surgeons. Yet as a Black woman I was aware that I had no margin for error. Rosalyn Yalow, a Nobel Prize winner in physics, is reported to have had a plaque in her office with a quote from Charlotte Whitton: "Whatever women do they must do twice as well as men to be thought half as good. Luckily, this is not difficult." I was constantly aware of the need for me to be twice as good as the men and of the different standards by which I was judged. I was aware that I represented all women and probably all Blacks. For most of my residency I felt isolated and vulnerable, a Shark on the Jets' turf; there was no one who reacted to residency as I did, no one who felt my discomfort, my fear, my sense of alienation. There was no one with whom to share my reality. And, in fact, exhaustion and denial were powerful states of being that allowed me to distance myself from the reality of my experiences.

I sometimes describe myself as "a general surgeon in recovery." When I completed training I went to work with a single-minded devotion to my profession and my family.

It took me about seven years before I came out of my trance and was able to look at myself and see how medical school, and especially residency, had affected and changed me. I had been so totally immersed, so completely in denial, that I had not recognized residency as a process of socialization, an initiation into a secret society — and I had been alien enough that the cloak of socialization had never totally covered me.

These realizations brought me to a turning point. Now I could start to reflect on my experiences, understand them, make meaning of them, and grow. Part of this process meant conceding the pain and trauma of the past. Another part — and equally significant — was my meeting another Black woman general surgeon who was at about the same place in her process of self-awareness. She was the first Black woman general surgeon with whom I could identify, the first person I met whose experiences were similar to mine. She was able to acknowledge and reflect on the trauma of her training years. She was a mirror for my reality, and I for hers. Our relationship was immensely validating and powerful. It was also a catalyst for healing.

As my healing began, I became curious about other African American women general surgeons. What was their experience of residency? Did it have an impact on who they are? How were our experiences alike and different? My research presented in this book represents the stories of six Black female surgeons, but it also tells my story — and possibly the stories of other surgeons who are not Black, or who are not female. And in the telling, it opens the door to understanding.

Chapter 2

What's Been Studied About Women and Minorities in Medicine

Historically, White men have been the subjects of medical research. From studies of the impact of various medications, to studies of normal anatomy and physiology, to studies looking at medical training, the focus has been on White males. For the purposes of those studies, men and women of color and White women were thought to be too complex; they posed too many variables that couldn't be controlled. There was an implicit acceptance of the White male as the normal standard, and an overt belief that the results of these studies could be generalized to all people — women and men of color, and White women. We now realize that White men do not represent all people and that even White males' understanding is enhanced by understanding the experiences of diverse individuals.[1]

Women are entering the profession of medicine in increasing numbers. Even surgery, long a male domain, is drawing more women. There is beginning to exist a body of literature on the impact of women on medicine, but little is known about the impact of medicine on women physicians.[2] Similarly, there is little in the literature about physicians of color, particularly women physicians of color.[3] Black women general surgeons represent a subset that has been paid scant attention, yet they are an important group that lives at the intersection of race, gender, and male privilege. Understanding their residency experiences provides insight into one of the most difficult professional initiations imaginable.

Most studies of women medical students and physicians tend to focus on the demographics of women physicians, the lack of women in medicine and the issues confronting women choosing medical careers. There are fewer personal reports or stories of the effects of medical education and training on the individual woman.

Even less is found in the literature regarding the demographics and experiences of Black physicians, or exploring the interfaces of race and gender in medical education and training. The few articles that do exist look at experiences of minorities; performance of minority students; historical perspectives and biographies of pioneering physicians of color, or demographics.

Women in Medical School and Practice

Historically, little research has focused on the intersection of gender with medical education and residency training experiences. One article noted, "Most studies that focused on women in medicine used students as subjects, and we have not found any studies of women residents."[4] Recently, with increasing numbers of women entering and graduating from medical schools, there has been more interest in women students, residents, and practicing physicians. "Women comprised only 7.7% of all physicians in 1970, whereas by the year 2010 they are expected to represent 30% of the total physician population."[5]

The conflicts inherent for women entering a medical career were studied by Notman and Nadelson. They noted:

> All [medical] students share a common goal — to develop an identity as a physician. The woman student has an additional task; she must define her identity as a woman in a "man's world" and cope with the myths about her ability to remain "feminine" and be a doctor.[6]

They identified other issues, including hostility directed toward women students; isolation and loneliness; guilt and sense of masquerading; and a lack of role models.

There is increasing interest in women physicians in practice. These studies tend to look at demographic information; satisfaction with practice and the profession of medicine; balancing multiple roles; experiences of gender discrimination; and the impact of increasing numbers of women on the profession of medicine, or some combination of these topics.

Minorities in Medicine

There is relatively little in the literature about minorities in medicine, and less about Black women physicians. Some researchers have addressed the shortage of minority physicians in academic medicine by reviewing barriers and opportunities. Others have studied residents' experiences of racial or ethnic discrimination; effects of certain student and institutional characteristics on minority medical student specialty choice; and performance of minorities.[7] None of these studies have addressed gender.

Black Women Physicians

Goodwin looked at the demographics of Black women in medicine, historical perspectives, and health policy concerns. She noted:

> In 1981, less than 5% of all physicians-in-training in the United States were Black. According to the Association of American Medical Colleges, for the academic year 1983–1984, the total number of Black students in the 127 medical schools in the United States was 3,892, out of a total of 56,167, or 7%.[8]

She documented the increasing numbers of women admitted to medical schools and stated that this increase seems to have occurred, at least in part, at the expense of overall minority admissions. "In the academic year 1983–1984, 44.9% of Black medical students were women (as compared to 29.4% among White students)." Goodwin expressed concern that this shift in demographics may result in "an even greater scarcity of Black physicians in those specialties which continue to be overwhelmingly male-dominated, such as surgery and the surgical specialties."

The Black woman physician was also discussed by Epps, who reviewed the history of Black women in medicine. She noted the lack of literature available about Black women physicians, and reviewed some of the concerns of women physicians. She expressed concern about the lack of Black female role models for Black women physicians, and the disconnection of Black women physicians from support systems in Black communities, which may result in professional and social isolation.[9]

Women in Surgery

The majority of women physicians are found in a small group of specialty areas.

> In a phenomenon that has come to be known as "clustering," about 60% of all women physicians are in five specialties that contain only about 40% of male physicians: pediatrics, psychiatry, family practice, internal medicine, and obstetrics-gynecology.[5]

Women continue to be underrepresented in the surgical specialties. A 1975 report noted that the number of "active women surgeons" in general surgery had increased from 311 in 1970 to 454 in 1974. More recent reports noted the continued increase in the number of women in general surgery. In 1970, fewer than one percent of general surgeons were women. By 1990, the number grew to more than six percent and at the present rate of increase it will approach ten percent by the year 2000. A U.S. government report noted, "In 1989–90, women comprised one in five surgical residents." The total number of general surgeons certified annually has remained relatively constant at about 950 per year. In the ten years prior to 1993, certification was achieved by 9,445 general surgeons. Approximately 60 percent of these will go on to do additional training in a subspecialty that requires general surgery as a prerequisite.[10] Moore and Priebe documented the relative youth of women surgeons:

> Although the longer training program in surgery resulted in a lower percentage of board-certified practitioners in the younger age groups, most women in surgical fields were in the youngest age groups. A recent breakdown of women surgeons in the United

States according to age showed that about 37% of all women surgeons at work in the surgical fields were still in their residency years, and another 8.5% were full-time staff or clinical fellows. In 1987, 52.6% of all women surgeons were under the age of 35, and 31.3% were from 35 to 44 years old; 84% of all women in surgical fields were under the age of 44.[11]

Researchers have been interested in "the surgical personality" and qualities that lead medical students to select a career in surgery; predictors of surgical skills; and personality traits.

McNamara looked at how women choose surgery, and the impact women have had on the field. She reported on the frequency with which women elect not to enter surgery despite preferring it.

Medical students frequently chose a specialty other than the one they preferred. Surgery was the first choice of 14.8% of men and the first preference of 22.3%. In contrast, 4.7% of women chose surgery while 15% preferred it. Thus, 66% of men who preferred surgery chose it while only 31% of women who preferred it pursued it as a career.[12]

She suggested that the choice of surgery is influenced by role model availability, the prevailing attitude of the profession, and training opportunities. Cohen, Woodward, and Ferr found that women students reported more barriers to career development then did men. Barriers included lack of support systems needed to combine career with family, lack of female role models, being taken less seriously than men, and sexism.[13]

Another identified barrier influencing the entry of women into surgery is the association of a "male style of behavior" with surgery.

Another inhibition to women's considering careers in surgery may be a prevailing belief that women cannot perform in surgery as well as men. In the Montreal Gazette, in 1889, a distinguished McGill professor declared, "Women may be useful in some departments of medicine, but in difficult work, in surgery, for instance, they would not have the nerve." This way of thinking persists today, and may be influencing young women into thinking that they have not got "what it takes."[14]

Ortiz looked at the "process of professional incorporation" in medical school and residency for women. One of her subjects was a woman surgical resident who was presented as being an exemplar of one way of incorporation into the surgical culture. "Beyond the normal problems faced by any neophyte of gaining peer status in a newly chosen social group, Dr. Masters had to resolve the dilemma of being a woman in a man's world. This was accomplished by two concurrent strategies: overt denial of the feminine role and the maximization of the doctor role."[15]

In a more recent study of surgical residents, researchers found that women and men residents had similar concerns about a number of aspects of the residency. These included numbers of hours worked, personal finances, length of education, and quality of education. There were six items for which women displayed higher levels of concern than their male colleagues: a) availability of role models, mentors, or both; b) comfort with expressing emotions at work; c) initiating personal relationships; d) maintaining personal relationships; e) having children during residency; and f) postponing family plans.[16]

In Scotland, women make up less than one percent of the general surgeons. Researchers there reported the results of a survey of thirty-five women surgeons working in Scotland. They concluded that the underrepresentation of women in surgery may be a result of discrimination, lack of time for children, and a lack of role models. A paper examining the role of women physicians in U.S. medicine noted that factors contributing to the dearth of women in surgical leadership in the U.S. include the lack of role models and an unwelcoming climate. The underrepresentation of women surgeons in academia and leadership roles is examined in other studies.[17]

Researchers have documented the characteristics of women surgeons — age, marital status, parental status, board certification, etc. — and the challenges they face. Several articles have been published on pregnancy during graduate medical training and surgical residencies. Studies have noted a disparity in the earnings of male and female surgeons and the continued existence of gender-related problems, despite an increasing number of women in general surgery.[18]

Black Women in Surgery

While the number of White women in surgery is increasing, there are still relatively few Black women in this field. A government report on graduate medical education noted:

> Although the percentage of women in medical school increased by nearly 25% from 1990 to 1993, women from ethnic and racial minority groups are still underrepresented in the medical student population. Less than 15% of the women enrolled in medical school in 1993–94 were from ethnic or racial minority groups. The largest underrepresented group was

African-American women, who comprised 11% of total enrollment of women.[5]

One surgical researcher stated, "Any discussion of Black women surgeons would be brief, and at best, anecdotal, as the number of Black women surgeons is exceedingly small (.0005% of all general surgeons)."[19]

The one research study that looks at Black women surgeons is the chapter by Sterling, in Organ and Kosiba's *A Century of Black Surgeons*. This chapter reviews the demographics, climate and general experience of this group of women. Sterling interviewed sixteen Black women surgeons and asked them "...about their motivation to become surgeons; who their role models have been; what problems they experienced in medical school, residency, and practice; whether any support systems have been available to them; and perhaps most important, what advice they would give to those young women contemplating surgery as a career."

The information provided about training for those women is succinct:

> Throughout their training and later as they started their practices, the women with whom I spoke all felt that as a surgeon they were discriminated against more often because of their sex than because of their race. The "boys' club" attitude of most male surgeons made it difficult for female surgeons to be respected professionally. Many chose to practice in a group after solo practice became too difficult from the perspective of referrals as well as from covering a practice twenty-four hours a day. Those involved in academic medicine also expressed concern about problems with promotion and opportunity that were attributed more to gender than to race.[19]

My search of the literature, while fascinating, provided me with little information about Black women surgeons and nothing about the impact of surgical training on the individuals experiencing it. All the materials reviewed are cited in the endnotes for this chapter.

Chapter 3

What Surgical Residencies Are Like

Medical students are exposed to surgery during their third and fourth years by spending time ("rotations" or "clerkships") working with residents on hospital surgical services. Medical students wanting to become general surgeons must have at least five years of supervised training after graduation from medical school. This period of training is called residency, because, at one time, physicians in training actually resided in the hospital. During residency, the teaching physicians, called "attendings," supervise the trainees and allow them increasing responsibility in caring for patients and performing operations.

Some residency training programs are very competitive, and made even more so by having a pyramidal design. At the base of the pyramid are the first- and second-year residents, who compete with each other for the more senior positions. For example, there may be 15 first-year residents, ten second-years, five third-year residents, and three residents in each of the fourth and fifth years. Some of the first- and second-year residents are planning to go into one of the surgical subspecialties — like orthopedics or otolaryngology — but need a year or two of general surgery as a base of experience. Others may want to continue on, and have to compete with their colleagues for a more senior position. Surgical residents' lives revolve around learning to perform operations, or "cases." Residents need to have experience in a variety of cases before they graduate from the program.

One of the responsibilities of residency is to "take call" — to be available to take care of any new admissions to the surgical service or any emergencies that might arise. Residents who are not on call "sign-out" — discuss their patients — with the call person so that if a problem arises, the call resident has some familiarity with the patient. Call responsibilities are in addition to the normal daily responsibilities of surgery and patient care. Call schedules generally range from every second night to every fourth night. The most junior residents take call in the hospital, while senior residents and attendings take call from home and may get called in to the hospital if their presence is needed. For some junior residents, it may be a source of pride to be able to handle emergencies well enough that they rarely have to call in the senior resident or attending.

Surgical residencies are known for their rigor. It has been said of residency:

> Traditionally surgical training has been highly inten-
> sive and very successful. The residency has been a true
> rite of passage, with the criteria for success being those
> of physical stamina and total commitment to a single
> goal as well as intellectual and technical proficiency.[1]

Surgeons are characterized as demanding, imperious, obsessive-compulsive, and perfectionistic. "A frenetic existence is regarded as the hallmark of a good surgeon."[1] Another researcher said about surgery:

> It is claimed that surgery attracts egotistical and domi-
> neering personalities — blowhards who need to be in
> command of the situation as "king of the castle" —

and, in fact, that the specialty reinforces these qualities: The program itself causes surgeons to become
arrogant and cocky. It's not a congenial atmosphere
like that of [internal] medicine. Most surgeons are
hard; they work long hours and they'll jump all over
you and chew you out. In such an environment
you develop that compulsive, rat-race, competitive,
aggressive personality.[2]

The effect of this environment on women has been the
subject of relatively little research. The increased interest in
the demographics of women in surgery and the impact of
increasing numbers of female surgeons on the profession has
been noted above, but the impact of the profession on the
women has rarely been considered. A review of the history of
women in surgery quoted Marie Mergler, the dean of Woman's
Hospital Medical College of Chicago in 1899.

> No woman studying medicine today will ever know
> how much it has cost the individuals personally con-
> cerned in bringing about these changes; how eagerly
> they have watched new developments and mourned
> each defeat and rejoiced with each success. For with
> them it meant much more than success or failure for
> the individual, it meant the failure or success of a
> grand cause.[3]

One researcher reported the results of interviews with thir-
teen practicing women surgeons, focusing on their residency
experience. She noted:

> The women acknowledged that the surgical residency
> poses different sets of problems for women who enter
> an essentially unknown, male-dominated environment
> and who must manage the tricky balance between a

professional and a family life. While they agree that the residency is tough, the women universally agree that the residency period needs to be tough to hone decision-making skills and technical surgical proficiency and to prepare surgeons for the real world of clinical practice.[4]

These women appeared to justify the isolation, demands, mental and physical exhaustion, and experiences of gender discrimination as experiences necessary to practice surgery.

> In the end, the residency prepares surgeons for the situations they will encounter in their actual, day-to-day practice. The surgical residency is a "microcosm of what one meets later in one's professional life," Margaret Dunn, MD, FACS, a general surgeon from Dayton, OH, observed. "The surgical residency compresses so many experiences into so little time, it is the most fundamental experience in the life of a surgeon; it affects your professional behavior and values. There aren't any residencies at this point that provide warm, sensitive, nurturing environments to men or women, but one does not encounter that kind of environment in one's professional life. The residency is just a reflection of the kinds of behaviors and attitudes one encounters later in one's career," Dr. Dunn concluded.[4]

There was agreement by the women surgeons interviewed that there is room for improvement in surgical residencies. "The residency is tough, but a surgical residency has to toughen you up somewhat. It doesn't, however, have to be a trial by fire," Dr. Kemeny said. They suggested ways that the stress of residency could be reduced: for example, by having ancillary personnel such as physicians' assistants take over some of the residents' task-oriented duties. The researchers commented on the need for psychological support for residents:

> [I would like] to build in opportunities for communication between residents and attendings, men and women, in terms of dealing with their feelings when a patient dies and relating to patients and families in crisis situations. I think both men and women surgical residents need to know that they can open up a chink in the armor of their feelings and proceed to function effectively, even superbly, as a surgeon.[4]

Some researchers have compared the concerns of male and female residents, and one reported on women residents' concerns about the lack of role models and mentors — challenges their male colleagues don't face. An article in the *Association of Women Surgeons Newsletter* advised members "How to swim with sharks: a primer."[5] They noted that "so much of the advice seems appropriate for women surgeons today." A more personal reflection on the nature of surgical residency and practice is provided by Dr. Kinder. She questioned whether or not the problems facing female surgeons are different from those facing the men.

> First, on a superficial level, a career of surgery poses terrific problems for everyone. The rigors of residency alone, with the long hours, the stress and frustration of a constant sense of inadequacy, the responsibility of decision-making under pressure, require the development of new personal resources if one is to achieve a balanced professional equanimity.... The concrete problems of men and women in surgery may be the same, but the problem-solving attitudes are often quite different.[1]

Kinder noted the differences between "early women in surgery" and current residents. She stated that female surgical pioneers:

> ...forced their way into the profession, wanted the same challenge and excitement that men found, and were willing, even eager, to play by the same rules. If we women reflected at all [on the long hours and sacrifice of a more balanced lifestyle], we concluded that total commitment was necessary in order to be an excellent surgeon.[1]

This is in contrast to the way she described women entering surgical programs at the time the article was written:

> These women do not see the selection of surgery as a choice between marriage and motherhood and a career: They intend to, and believe that they can, do it all. They have no hesitation in saying in an interview that they plan to have a family (something the rest of us never would have considered doing). They are outspoken about what they believe are the inappropriate rigors of the traditional residency, the every-other-night-on-call schedule, the macho "I can take it" persona of the surgeon. The things the rest of us, men and women alike, identified as virtues, these young women see as perversions of the well-balanced, thoughtful, and caring professional the ideal surgeon should be.[1]

Kinder went on to suggest that a change in the metaphors about the way we perceive surgery may be instrumental in preserving the good elements and allowing appropriate change. It may well be that women surgeons will provide those new metaphors.

Chapter 4

African American Women
General Surgeons Tell Their Stories

"In a good surgeon:
a hawk's eye,
a lion's heart,
and a lady's hands."

~ Wright, 1589

My research had two parts: an initial survey of all identified African American general surgeons, and in-depth interviews with a selected group of participants. I used the survey to get background information about this group of physicians and to identify women who were potential interview participants. The methods used to conduct the surveys and interviews are discussed in Chapter 6. I mailed surveys to 110 women who were identified as a result of letters sent to surgical and medical professional organizations and by word of mouth as being Black women general surgeons. The categories of responses are displayed on the following page.

Survey Results

# SURVEYS MAILED	110	% OF TOTAL SURVEYS
# Accounted for	49	45
Undeliverable	12	11
White women	6	5
Men	1	1
Total # without data	19	17
Total # with data*	30	27 ** (61% of completed surveys)
Resident	12	40
Fellow	2	
<5 years out	3	
Subspecialist	2	
Retired	1 ***	
Not practicing	1	
The researcher	1	
Eligible for interview	8 **** (26% of completed surveys)	

  * Of the 30 surveys with data, not all included responses to every question
  ** One incomplete response
 *** Survey not completed
**** One response returned after interviews completed

Age

The age range of respondents varied from 29 years to "10 years post-retirement." The median age was 37, the mean age 36. There were twelve women between 29 and 35; nine women 36 to 40; five women between 41 and 45; one woman between 46 and 50; one woman over 50; and two who did not identify their ages. As would be anticipated, the younger women were still in residency.

Parents' Occupations

Five women had physician fathers; two of these fathers were surgeons. Other occupations included minister, musician, engineer, mailman, taxi driver, pharmacist, policeman, auto mechanic, airplane mechanic, biochemistry professor, electrician, and sales executive (Appendix F). None of the mothers were physicians, but seven had professions within medicine, including nurse's aide, LPN, RN, RN practitioner, pharmacist, and medical administrator (Appendix G).

Parents' Education

Thirty parents had at least some college and five had not completed high school.

Undergraduate Education

These women attended a wide range of undergraduate institutions, with four (13%) attending traditionally Black colleges. Five women (17%) graduated from Ivy League schools. One woman was educated outside the United States for both undergraduate and medical school (Appendix H).

Medical Education

Two of the women attending Black undergraduate schools also attended Black medical schools. Three women who attended White undergraduate schools chose to attend Black medical schools. Three women attended Ivy League medical schools (Appendix I).

Residency

Most women left their medical schools to do their residency training. Four women who attended Black medical schools chose traditionally Black residency programs (Appendix J).

Influences

There were a wide variety of reasons given for entering surgery. Many said that they enjoyed surgery the most of all specialties, others cited their medical school role models or experiences in surgery as being instrumental, some noted the immediate gratification aspects of surgery, and many liked the technical aspects (Appendix K).

The survey results were used to identify surgeons whom I could interview about their residency experiences. I wanted to speak with African American women who were five to 15 years out of residency training and who were currently practicing general surgery. At the time I was doing the interviews, I had identified seven women— three on the East Coast and two on the West Coast. One woman was so busy that I was never able to make an appointment to talk with her. Another woman sent her survey back after I had completed the interviews and compiled the information.

We will first meet the participants, and then look more closely at their composite residency experiences.

Diane

Diane initially planned to be a pediatrician, until as a medical student she did her pediatric rotation and "hated it!" She liked surgery but was initially put off by the thought of six years of residency. The institution she selected for her training was nonpyramidal and seemed to be less "back-stabbing" and more "mellow" than the pyramidal programs she considered. They also had finished more women than some of the other programs. Yet, graduating from her residency in 1985, she was the first Black woman to complete the program.

It is her impression that gender was more of an issue than race, although race may have, at times, been an issue.

Even though there were several women that finished before me, there is still such a longstanding, ingrained sense that surgery is a field for men. The women were not treated overtly differently but that attitude was always there. Attendings would think that a woman couldn't do a long case because she was not tough enough to stick it out for the six or eight hours. It was apparent by the attitudes that they displayed. There was also a tendency to lump all the women together. The worst part about that was that a year ahead of me there was one woman who was truly terrible. She came in the midst of a series of women who had actually been pretty good, but she set us back 50 years. On almost every rotation I would be following wherever she had just been, and I always had to reestablish that women are credible and know what they're doing. I always felt that I had to prove myself by doing a better job than the people that came before me and had to lay the groundwork for the people coming after me.

There were a couple of Black men that were in the program for several years before leaving for other programs, and I didn't get the sense that they were having as much resistance from the attendings about giving up cases. When I compared my experiences with the White women in the program they seemed to have the same complaint as I. But it's always hard to know how much of the male residents' talk was just bragging rather than real.

Overall, the attendings were pretty good to me. There had been a Black male who had finished the program

years earlier and I guess they'd gotten over being concerned about race at that point. You know, it wasn't
a takeover because it was just me, and I was very non-
threatening. But for some of the patients it was a
shock. They would look at me like, "Who are you?"
and say things like, "Are you sure you're not a nursing student?" There were no big incidents but you
could just get that sense when you walked in the room
that the patient was thinking, "This is really not what
I was expecting."

Diane also felt a need to prove herself by being tough.

> Our motto every day with sign-out was always, "Call
> me if you need me, but to call is a sign of weakness." I
> can honestly say that in six years, I don't think I ever
> called anybody in. Although many of the guys did. But
> I just knew that it would be seen as my ultimate failure
> if I called anyone in. So I never did. There were prob-
> ably plenty of times when, in retrospect, I should have.
> I developed that sense of toughness. The knowledge
> that I really could take care of things myself. But part
> of it was getting to the point where no one could say
> that I didn't have the stamina to finish because I was a
> woman. I knew that there were different standards so
> that if a man called it must have been really, really bad,
> but if I called it would show that I was weak.

Despite the value of toughness, one of the characteristics
Diane valued in her residency program was the low-key atmosphere. The attending surgeons there were less aggressive than
other surgeons she had worked with. "They kept up with the
literature and quietly did a pretty good job and had good
reputations, but they weren't out there handing out business
cards and saying, 'I'm the greatest surgeon in America.'"

Diane found ways to take care of herself during her residency and to stay true to herself.

> We had two weeks of vacation a year but usually no money to go anywhere. I tended to hibernate at home or go to the nearest beach. I was just so grateful that for two weeks I could turn my beeper off. Once you leave the hospital it's like you're starting life over.
>
> At one point a friend of mine in Anesthesia and I bought ballet subscription tickets. Every so often we would say, "That's it. We're leaving. We're going to the ballet. Good-bye!" It was nice to remember that there really was such a thing. Nice to do something that was totally unrelated to what you do every day.
>
> I also read a lot. I've always been a big reader, so I would always find something to read in those moments when the call was not horrible. And it was not going to be medical.
>
> My friends didn't see me as changed after training. Most of them still don't really believe that I do what I do.

Looking back, Diane feels that more mentoring would have improved her residency experience.

> When I finally got to the point of almost finishing, there were times when I would be with some of the junior women. I could get a sense of helping them along with some of the mundane, day-to-day things. They were things that had puzzled me to no end but at the time I really had nobody to help me. These women were able to talk it out and realize that, "OK, this too will pass. It's just a phase. They don't hate

you personally, they really are a little bit less likely to give you a case, and in the end you will have done so many cases that you really don't care. It just seems like it matters right now, today, that you didn't do this hernia, but you're not going to have a dearth of hernias in your lifetime."

The female attendings did not really act as mentors for us. They were busy and our only contact was right there at the OR table. They were also trying to establish themselves since they were probably the only two women surgeons in town. They were paving their own way, establishing themselves and building their reputations.

At the completion of her six years of residency Diane felt well prepared for practice.

There were few things that you were going to go out in private practice and have to deal with that you hadn't had a good preparation for. General surgeons are usually pretty independent and have to be pretty flexible. We have to be able to deal with whatever we find. You can't go into an operation with a nice fixed plan, because in spite of all the diagnostic tests there may be some totally unforeseen problem for which you have to be able to think on your feet and come up with a good solution. It was very satisfying to watch the attendings recognize over time that I was competent and defer to my opinion about what to do. I recognized that it had been a long battle but finally the attending realized that I did learn how to operate and that he didn't need to watch me every second anymore.

One of the things Diane did not feel well prepared for was dealing with emotionally charged patient situations.

> That was probably the area for which we had the least preparation. It was tough the first time I had to go tell somebody that their breast biopsy was cancer and tell them their options. We didn't get the experience of doing it at all in residency. There wasn't much of a clinic patient population and with mostly private patients the resident was often a ghost surgeon and the attending was the one with the relationship with the patient.
>
> There was also no assistance in dealing with those experiences internally. Because, you know, men don't deal with that stuff. Their attitude was more like, "They died and it wasn't your fault. It was a good day." Since we didn't have a lot of pre- and post-operative contact with the patients, we were pretty insulated from many of those experiences. If a patient had a long and lingering illness you might have them on your service for a long period of time and end up interacting with the family a lot. Then you could see the residents trying to withdraw. They'd round [check on the patient] when the family was not there [so they could] get in and out as quickly as possible. You could tell it was a drain emotionally on them but it was very much an unaddressed set of issues.

Although Diane found her residency to offer a "nice balance of being low-key and still providing enough experience," she thinks that there needs to be more attention paid to the "people skills side of surgery."

That's why all these people finish and they go out in the world and they're immediately obnoxious to every patient that they meet. It's because no one has ever really taught them that you have to talk, that the patient is not a case. They don't seem to understand that the breast cancer might actually have a job that's about to be downsized and that they have other concerns besides how convenient is this timing for the surgeon's lifestyle. They don't realize that for patients every surgery is like the biggest decision of their life. It's not like you can just go in and give them five minutes of your time and expect them to be willing to sign.

Diane acknowledges the internal strength needed to complete a surgical residency. She describes her residency experience as being like scuba diving.

It's like you're submerged for a long period of time trying to get some particular goal or prize and then you finally get to come up for air. You know right at the beginning that it's going to be a dive and that you're going to have to go through a long, generally unpleasant period of time but, hopefully, that it's going to be worth it at the end. That you will have obtained some set of skills that will last your lifetime. And that you have done it pretty much without a lot of help.

Once you come up for air you start thinking of a million reasons not to go back down there. I understand why they only gave you two weeks of vacation — if you had an extra week your brain would start to say, "Wait a minute now. Why am I going back?" You'd have just enough time for your brain to reset and say, "Hmmm."

Janice

It was like boot camp to me. It was like a very isolated boot camp. I didn't get support from my colleagues or from the faculty. As an attending now I try and always encourage the medical students to come in and we talk. One medical student, she's actually pregnant, wants to do a surgical residency. We talk about that and we look at this...look at that. I can't remember any attending, when I was a resident, that I could go to and say, "I'm having problems with this, or I just feel this way, or this is what's going on." There was no one that I would even have thought of telling that I had a bad day or a bad case, or whatever. There was no one that I would reveal that kind of thing to. So for me it was like boot camp. It was real isolated and my support came from my family. I didn't turn to my colleagues, because it was a pyramidal program. Even though there was no outward pulling people down, you knew that it was either you or me, and eventually somebody was going to get cut, and it wasn't going to be me. So there was an almost subliminal feeling that you really couldn't get support from the people there.

Janice did her residency in a pyramidal program, that is, a program where there were a large number of junior residents who competed for a few chief resident positions. She experienced this as creating an atmosphere of intense competition and the need to maintain the appearance, if not the reality, of perfection. Janice felt that exhibiting her fatigue, loneliness, need for companionship, need for family connections, emotion, and the like was viewed as a demonstration of weakness.

The most difficult of Janice's experiences during residency followed a car accident.

> I was in a car accident at the end of my intern year and had a head injury, and missed about three and a half months of work. In trying to recover from that it took me a long time to get back. Even though I went back to work after about three months I wasn't the way I was before my injury. There was clearly a difference, and it took a very long time to recover from that. It wasn't that someone could look at me and say, "Oh, you were hurt in a car accident." But I had a lot of trouble with my memory and with reading and concentrating, and things like that. And that was real tough for me because I was going into my second year and I had a lot of anxiety because it was a pyramidal program. Although I had done well my first year, the cut really had two more cuts left. I really was concerned that my performance maybe would have suffered. So it was very anxiety-provoking for me to go through that and try and deal with my personal recovery from the accident. And there were people who used that. There were people who said, "She'll never be a surgeon. You know, we should probably cut her. She'll never be able to operate." No one said it to my face, but it came out to me later that certain people made these comments. That was hard when I found that people I thought were supportive for me really weren't. It was really kind of a dog-eat-dog kind of atmosphere.

In that atmosphere, Janice saw that women who did not fit into the expected mold suffered consequences.

> When I was a third-year resident, there was an intern who was married and got pregnant very shortly after

she started her internship year. We all knew she was going to get cut, and she did. Women who were pregnant in the residency had a difficult time. It was a very competitive and very demanding — physically demanding — residency, and so no one was willing to help out. No one wanted to take extra call. If a woman was pregnant and had to go on maternity leave, the attitude of the other residents was, "Well, I've got to take more call now." It was very evident. It didn't affect me directly because I wasn't in that position, but it was clear that if you were in that position it must have been extremely difficult. There was one chief resident who miscarried in her second trimester. We all really thought it was due to the stress. There was not the support to take care of yourself. For example, if you're a chief resident you probably don't need to do the last three breast biopsies. You could go take a rest. But that kind of support was not evident. You were expected to always be there, always be ready, always perform, never get sick, never need time off, never need to take care of yourself.

Janice's program was in a traditionally Black institution, and she felt that race had little impact, but even though there had been several women graduates of the program before she finished in 1991, the competitiveness was complicated by her gender. "As far as being female, there was a real need to show that I could do as good a job, and probably a better job, than some of the male colleagues."

The push to prove herself was demonstrated by a story Janice related.

I did a case when I was an intern with a cardiothoracic surgeon. We were doing a decortication [cutting away scar tissue] and we were taking down some of the adhesions and he wanted me to Bovie [cauterize] on my finger. To put my finger under the blade. You can do that for a little while and then it gets pretty hot. When I told him that it was burning my finger, his response was, "Oh, come on, Janice, you can't take it?" and would he have said that if I was a guy? Well, I don't know, but I took it and I had burns on my hands just because I thought that I needed to show that I could do it. And that if I didn't do it, it would be looked upon as though I was a woman and I couldn't do it, not because it was just a hot Bovie.

From the time of her decision to be a surgeon on through her interviews for residency positions, Janice was aware of being treated differently because she was a woman:

As a medical student I didn't get support from the clinical faculty to do surgery but I wasn't told by any of them, "You shouldn't do this." It was really on my interviews that I started to get this impression that men really would try and do what they could to discourage you from doing a surgical residency. There were those kinds of comments, you know…the stuff about family. "When are you going to have kids?" And all that kind of stuff.

I remember when interviewing, I was asked how did I know I was strong enough to be a surgeon? When I look back on it now I have probably half a dozen answers that I could give, but at the time you're very inexperienced in how to handle those kinds of situations, and you want to be a surgeon so you want to say the right thing. You don't want to piss people off.

These kinds of experiences had an ongoing impact for her

throughout her residency:

> I remember one of the attendings. The reason why I
> always wear a T-shirt under my scrubs is because
> scrubs are not cut for women and so when you lean
> forward...men used to...you could tell they were
> looking down your shirt. It happened all the time. It
> was those kinds of inappropriate behavior that the
> male residents don't have to deal with. You would
> have to wonder, am I wearing too big of a shirt? Do I
> need a safety pin? You can't bend over and take care
> of the patient who's bleeding on the floor without
> worrying about somebody looking down your shirt.
> The male residents didn't have to deal with that.

For Janice, her residency experiences become clearer in
retrospect. She is now in a position to work with medical
students and residents, and in observing how they are treated
she gains insight into her own experiences.

> We see stuff here all the time. There's no question
> that it's sexist. Things like inequality in the call sched-
> ule distribution so that female residents either get put
> with weak residents consistently or get holiday time
> on call and weekend time on call, whereas other
> people don't. They're berated more on rounds, given
> more scut to do. Expectations are different for them.
> Small infractions are made into huge things. You can
> see the pattern now. It's hard when you're in it, to
> know whether it's you, or is it because you're female,
> or is it something else? It's hard to sort that stuff out
> when you're in the middle of it, but when you sit back
> you know that you've been there, and you've seen
> that as a resident, and it comes out more clearly.

Even the transition from residency to post-residency training was influenced by being female. Despite the perception that Janice and the other female chief resident were the best residents finishing that year, she feels that they did not get the same level of support their male colleagues received.

> We were the two best residents — everybody said that — but there was not the support that we needed to do fellowship training afterwards. We both got fellowships on our own. It wasn't the situation where the attending who knows somebody picks up the phone and makes connections for you. Did that happen to the male residents? I knew a couple of male residents who did benefit from connections that the attendings had. Is that because of what they were interested in, or because they were men? I don't know, but it did seem that when the potential for the help to be given was there, it wasn't given.

After completing residency, Janice went to another institution to do a research fellowship. During her fellowship she was made aware of her unique position as a Black woman.

> At the university where I did my research fellowship, there were no women at all in the department. Never. And there had only been a few female residents. At the time there were no female residents and no female attendings. A lot of those guys had studied there in undergrad and in medical school, and they had never even seen a Black female surgeon. Never seen! So when I went there they were all, like...I mean, the jaws just hung open. It was amazing how the jaws just hung! Literally. They didn't realize how surprised they looked. And you know it, because you've seen that look before and you know what it feels like.

Janice learned to make accommodations to survive in this "boot camp" environment. The need to accommodate herself and remain alert to how carefully she was observed created burdens for Janice that her male colleagues did not share.

> I really tried to minimize my femaleness. I never wore pastel colors and never wore my hair out. I always had it back in a ponytail or up in a banana clip. I never wore long earrings. I always wore just small balls that would not be interpreted as unprofessional or nonprofessional. And if you wear makeup, are you sending the wrong message? Or are you just wearing makeup because you like to wear makeup? Or maybe because you're going somewhere when you leave. But that whole appearance thing was a real problem. I wanted people to look at me as a doctor and a surgeon and not a woman who is a surgeon. I didn't wear dresses. I was just all about surgery and I didn't want anything else to detract from the impression that I gave, as far as being able to do this.

Janice was aware that other women surgeons found different ways of accommodating to the pressures of being female in a male profession.

> I remember going to one of the national meetings and there were two presenters, both from the same program. One was a female fellow and the other was a female attending. When I listened to them talk they sounded like dolls. They had this high-pitched, weird, kind-of-like-offering-tea voice. And they both did it. This was not...you know, how you emulate things that you like about people? This was a learned behavior. This wasn't a coincidence. And this was in a White program where my impression was that they

still have this idea about what women should be and what position they should hold. It was like they thought that women should have a very submissive role. Their tone of voice and their demeanor was just so submissive. Actually one of them had been a Marine. She got up there with this little high-pitched voice. And in a room full of surgeons — all men — trying to appeal to something else...not being able to rely on your intelligence to get your point across.... It seemed that they thought that they needed to go through these other channels. It's unfortunate that women have to do that. You should be able to get up there and just talk without worrying about somebody saying, "Well, you're this, or you're that, or you're not female enough, or you're too female, or whatever." The audience should just be listening to what you're saying, because giving the talk is hard enough.

There were no female role models for Janice to look to that would enable her to find a new way to be a woman in a surgery residency. The prevailing ethos valued a macho dedication to the work over any type of human connection or need. Janice makes it clear that she devoted her heart and soul to becoming a surgeon.

I put everything on hold during residency. I was completely independent throughout my residency. I had no children. I had no other responsibilities and was very, very selfish for five years. I was willing to make the personal sacrifice because surgery was what I wanted. So even though you're up all night and you don't go home for Christmas, and you take call on New Year's, and you've got to work on Thanksgiving — those things were just a part of it.

This environment did take its toll, though, and in becoming such a successful resident in the "macho" male style Janice found herself distanced from her humanity. This was apparent in some of her interactions with other residents, and in the distance she took when dealing with difficult experiences like the death of a patient.

> I remember when I was a third-year resident on a really busy cardiothoracic service. My intern and I were coming in early every morning making rounds. It was just a really busy service. One weekend he asked me — it was a Saturday and we were getting ready to do an emergency open heart — and he asked me if he could go home, because he and his wife were moving. They were getting ready to have a new baby. And they were moving into their new apartment. And I told him, "Absolutely not! How can you? We have an emergency heart. How are you going to go home?" Because I knew I would have to pre-op the patient. "How are you going to go home?" And now, to this day, I feel so bad about that insensitivity. I just couldn't imagine how anyone else could put anything before surgery.

> When I was a resident I didn't have the human side. That was pushed back. I don't know that that's really a good thing to do. I think I did what I needed to do to get through the program. But I don't think I was very feminine or woman-like about it. I didn't have the other concerns. I didn't have the family, and the husband, and the other concerns. It was just surgery. And now that I have those things, my perspective is very different. Now there are other things that are more important to me, but during that time there really wasn't.

Despite the difficult working conditions, the benefits of becoming a surgeon justified the price Janice had to pay. From her first exposure to surgery as a medical student she fell in love with it.

> It's such an emotional high. It's so ego-gratifying when you feel like you've really done something. I guess when we come to medicine we all have whatever baggage we bring. We all do it for different reasons. And for me it was always about taking care of patients, and really...I don't know why I'm getting teary-eyed, but it's very emotional. It's very emotional because it's really about caring for patients and how when you lose patients and when you have things that don't work out the way you would want...how that affects you. For me, whenever I lost a patient, that was so hard for me.

Janice believes that she was changed by her residency and that it made her a better person, because being a physician can be a life-changing experience. Undergoing a residency, putting her life on hold, making personal sacrifices and then having a chance to reflect back on it had a significant impact on Janice both personally and professionally.

> It made me a better doctor because I was always trying to figure out what I would do different and how I could change something, but it also made me a different person because it allowed me really to appreciate the life part of it. I mean, we see suffering and pain and people dying all the time, and when you really take it into the context that it should be...of where your life is...that makes it different. So I think from that regard it changed me. I guess the surgery part of it made me, kind of, tougher. After I finished my

training I realized that there were things that I just would not compromise. That now that I had made it through there were things that I won't give up. Anything that has to do with my family comes first. I don't care if I'm on call. I have a kid. I don't put aside my family for surgery and I, before, would do that. So I guess it allowed me to realize what my priorities are. And that, even though surgery is very important to me and is very rewarding professionally and personally...I need both. I can't do the surgery without my family. I can't do one without the other. I really need time for both. It has helped me balance stuff.

The hard work of residency has paid off in more than one way. Janice is now in a position where she can identify sexism when she sees it and work to change things. She has the authority to positively influence the experience of women surgery residents as they go through their training in her institution.

So it's kind of retrospective. I think that the whole experience ends up making you a different person. For the women, I think it makes us better in that it allows us to help people who come behind us. For the men, I think it just propagates. I don't think they see what women have to deal with and what they may need during residency. This weakness thing is such an issue. Now, as an attending and as a person who has more authority, and this is without question based on my residency, I do give preference to female residents and medical students. I'm probably harder on male residents. Not that I let female residents slide, but I know that if I have a female resident or medical student and a male resident or medical student — exactly the same, identical, everything's the same, grades, references, everything — I'll pick the female just because she's female. And I would do that in a heartbeat. In any instance. And it's based on the fact that I know that it's not equal. We have more to deal with. We have more proving to do. And so I'm more likely to give guys a hard time and I'm probably more likely to be a female chauvinist when it comes to women residents. And that's unfortunate, I guess, for men. I don't know how you get around it. It's not meant to propagate what happened, but it's a retaliation, I think, in a way that doesn't necessarily hurt. It kind of gives males the experience of being on the firing line all the time. And the expectation to prove yourself and to be above whatever that baseline standard is, which is the standard which we had to live up to all the time.

In my ideal residency there would be support for the family. It's real simple stuff, like on-site child care. If you just had a baby and you want to breastfeed and do that during the day, or you just want to go and see your kid for lunch, you should be able to do that. There would also be more attention paid to time off for residents. Currently it's mandated that residents have to have at least one 24-hour period per week where they're not at all involved with patient care. It's not enough, but it's better than it used to be. I want to change the attitude that sees the need for family and personal time as a weakness: "You mean you want time off? You want to walk around the park? What, are you crazy?"

In the end, for Janice, the real payoff of her surgical residency is the joy and fulfillment she gets from being a surgeon. "When I was a medical student my first rotation was surgery and I just loved it. And when I did everything after that it just wasn't the same. Whenever I saw the surgeons coming down the hall I'd wish I was there." It is clear that Janice's love of surgery persists, even to the extent that she hopes her daughter will be a surgeon. And if her daughter does follow in her footsteps, it is likely that, because of people like Janice, her residency experience will be far more humane.

Joyce

Joyce thoroughly enjoyed her residency and missed it a lot after she finished. She completed her training in 1992 in the institution she had attended since undergraduate school. It was a program that had several other women, although no other Black women. Joyce experienced a sense of camaraderie and closeness among the five most senior residents, the chiefs. This may have been made possible by the less competitive nature of a non-pyramidal program.

It was also a program where the attending surgeons were supportive of the residents and developed personal relationships with them. "I think they treated me pretty well. I was competent and they could trust me to take care of the patients and tell them what was going on." Joyce particularly remembers her relationship with one of the attendings whom she visited after finishing the program.

> I was there at Thanksgiving time and I went to see Dr. S. who was at home after having had surgery for

pancreatic cancer. I called him up on the phone — and he's the kind of guy you'd call in the middle of the night and he'd answer on the first ring and say, "S." And you'd say, "Dr. S., I have an appendicitis in the ER." And that's all he wanted, just one sentence. And the next thing he'd say is, "What time?" You didn't call him if you didn't know what was going on.

Well, I called him when I got to town and he recognized my voice right away. He said, "Where are you?" I said, "I'm in town." He said, "Well, when are you coming to see me?" So I went to see him and he was upstairs in his bed. We were talking and I was a little uncomfortable because I didn't know when I was to leave, so I started up like I was getting ready to leave. He said, "Sit down! Where are you going? I'll tell you when to go." (Laughs) He was that kind of guy. Very much a mentor and very interested in teaching you.

There were no female attendings in Joyce's program but she did not experience that as a loss.

Along with the overall enjoyment of her training, Joyce experienced significant stress. "Just about everything I can think of was stressful — sick patients, patients dying. The whole thing was just stressful." The program did not provide support for residents who were dealing with difficult situations.

There was no discussion about how to deal with difficult clinical experiences like the death of a patient. I have several vivid memories. One Saturday morning a teenager came in after a dirt-bike accident. I went out and told the family and they just about attacked me. Another time a patient came in after a gunshot wound to the head and was brain dead. I told the family that he was dead but we were temporarily keeping him alive on a machine to let them think about donating his organs. They told me off right there and then! "Why are you keeping him alive! How dare you! Why are you trying to use his organs?"

In another episode the patient owned a little shop and some men came in and robbed him and shot him. I went upstairs to the family and told them that he had died in the OR and they started screaming and wailing. That was difficult enough, but the little lady that works in the business office there came out and told me off. "You people always come up here to talk to these families. They're always carrying on. Why don't you go somewhere else!" The family was screaming and she was screaming at me. Nobody ever tells you how to deal with that kind of thing.

I remember one event that really bothered me. I can still see her face. A girl came in on a Thursday morning. She was standing at the bus stop going to school, and got shot. A Black girl with long braids. She came into the ER and she was awake. She looked right at me and she said, "Please tell my mother I'm here." It was the last thing she said to me. She died in the OR. And I still can see that little girl — she was about sixteen. A pretty Black girl with braids and big eyes. And she looked up and said, "Please tell my mother I'm here." Oh, goodness! I still remember that.

Joyce learned to cope with these emotional experiences by putting them out of her consciousness.

I think I buried all that. It wasn't too hard to bury, because you're so busy. You're here talking to this family that somebody's dead and they're screaming, and your beeper is going off, and there is another crisis somewhere else that you need to attend to. I think there're a lot of unresolved crises inside of me. You just move on to the next one and then you've been up a day and a half and you fall asleep dead at the first opportunity. You don't even have time to think about it. It just ends up being swept away in the hustle.

The pace of life may also have kept Joyce from the awareness that she was being treated differently than the other residents because she was a Black female.

If I was treated differently, I didn't notice. I notice being treated differently a lot more now that I've been out of residency. It's a lot more obvious. I look back and I think it must have happened in residency too, and I just didn't pick up on it, or I kept it at a subconscious level and didn't react to it. Now it's like a light bulb went off in my head and I'm aware of how I'm treated differently. In residency there are so many people around, and so many layers of things, that people may not pick you out as readily as being unique. Also, in residency it's so busy and there's so much work to do that people almost don't care who is there. It's like, "I don't care who is taking over — I don't care if they're Black, Yellow, White — as long there is somebody to turn the beeper over to."

Joyce's current environment is different from her residency, and she recounts several experiences illustrating how she is sometimes treated.

Recently I was in the cafeteria at the hospital and one of the medical doctors came up to me and said, "I'm glad I ran into you. I sent you a patient who is going to come and see you. It's a Black lady named White. Ha, ha, ha, ha! Isn't that funny! It's a Black lady named White. Have you ever seen a Black lady named White?"

Another time I saw an elderly patient in the hospital with a colon cancer. We had a long conversation about his condition and the operation, and I did the surgery. Several months later he came to my office in follow-up. He was in tears. He said, "I just have to tell you this. When you first came into the room and said you were Dr. Joyce and wanted to do the surgery, I didn't want you to do my surgery because you were Black. I feel so bad, because everything turned out so well and you were so nice and everybody says good things about you. I just wanted to tell you that. You've changed my whole outlook."

One other experience involved an elderly Black lady who was hospitalized with a colon cancer. I said that the test showed cancer and that she needed to have surgery, and explained it all to her. She just kept looking at me. And finally she said, "Who's going to do the surgery?" I said, "I'm going to." She said, "Well, who's going to help you?" Actually she said, "Which man is going to help you?"

There was no seminal experience leading Joyce to become a surgeon. Surgery was something that she felt drawn to, something that she just "clicked with." Yet, she finds general surgeons, as a group, to be disappointing.

> Since I've finished residency, I've discovered that I don't really like general surgeons. Many of them give surgery a bad name. Many of the general surgeons here where I practice don't take care of sick patients post-operatively. And they're rude. They tend to think they're something special and important. It's almost like something that has been inbred.

As are her experiences in practice, Joyce's residency experiences were a mixture of the bitter with the sweet. She describes residency experience as having been like an orange.

> I like oranges and they're good to eat. When you get an orange you peel it from the top going around and around, holding it in your hand. And while you're peeling it sometimes the thing squirts and it gets in your eye and it burns. But you keep peeling it anyway because you want to eat the orange. Residency is kind of like peeling an orange and it burning you. And then you eat the orange and it's good. You can never get the orange smell off your hands once you peel it. It's good and enjoyable and tasty, but there are some parts of it that really smart.

Joyce, now almost 36, still wants to get married and have children, but at this time being a surgeon is just right.

> I would never go back and undo it. I'm really glad I'm doing it. I think I did the right thing. I think it is what God intended me to do. It just feels right. It's hard, but I really enjoyed my residency and I really enjoy my practice.

Marie

During the limited time available for Marie's interview, she offered a somewhat kaleidoscopic view of her residency. It was an experience she loved, and an atmosphere in which she felt she thrived. Yet she acknowledges that as the first Black female in her program, she had her share of difficulties and challenges.

> I had a lot of problems the first couple of years. Not so much from the faculty but the other residents sometimes, and also the patients. One of the big problems was the fact that I was a female and then that I was Black. There are stories that go on and on about, "Your doctor is not only Black, she's female...your doctor is not only female, she's Black." It kind of bounced on back and forth and it went on and on and on.

But these experiences occurred in a context full of excitement and richness. Marie trained with some of the best known surgeons of the time and took care of patients whose names would be familiar in most households. She experienced the surgeons as being supportive of her, teaching her well, mentoring her, and including her in their previously all-White male surgical society meetings and social gatherings.

From the time that she was a small child, Marie knew she wanted to be a physician and to help those who were less fortunate than herself. "I always knew I was going to be a doctor and I always knew I was going to be a surgeon." She acknowledges that there may have been times when she was treated differently than other residents were, but is not interested in dwelling on these.

> Now that I look back at it there were people that
> were difficult individuals, residents and attendings.
> There were attendings that may have used personal-
> ity things to disguise racism. During my residency I
> did not feel...but maybe I would not allow myself to
> feel. We're talking about somebody coming out of
> medical school in 1977 and being totally shocked that
> I'm going to be an educated Black woman. There
> could have been racism and sexism. There probably
> was, but I was so focused on doing what I felt needed
> to be done. And what I wanted to do was get some-
> where so I could be the best Goddamned surgeon for
> my people. That's me. Things that are unpleasant
> I ignore. That's me.

She presents herself as a person of great resolve and as
one unwilling to compromise patient care. These characteristics were useful to her during her residency training, when
she insisted on standing up for things that she knew to be
right. She gained a reputation for being an excellent surgeon
who would always do her best and who refused to take any
nonsense.

When things got rough during Marie's training, she dealt
with it by "just working harder" and accepting the difficult
times as opportunities to become a better person and physician. In some ways her surgical residency seemed tame to her
after her experiences as a high school student integrating her
Southern small-town high school. In talking about her residency, she minimizes any possibly negative experiences and
focuses on the positive aspects of her training.

Marie feels that the core of who she is was not altered by
her residency experiences. She has been strongly influenced

by values instilled in her by her mother. She states that before, during, and since her training, she has been the "backbone" of her family and very interested in helping others. She continues to find ways to be of service to others through teaching and being a role model as well as caring for patients. Marie feels that it was her upbringing that gave her the skills, communication ability, and compassion to cope with emotionally difficult situations in residency, such as the death of a patient. She also believes that these skills must be a part of one's upbringing and cannot be taught in a surgical residency program.

Marie does not believe that being a Black woman had an impact on her residency experience.

> My being a Black woman did not change how my attendings trained me. It did not make my experience different from that of my peers for either them or me. I don't think so at all. I enjoyed my residency. There were six months that were horrible, and it came to fruition a couple of years later what was wrong, and it was a particular senior resident.

She refuses to generalize about female or male surgeons, focusing rather on the personality characteristics unique to each individual. She sums up her philosophy of life as follows:

> Whether you're a surgeon or not, you've got to give whatever you do your best, and do it right in the best interest of everybody else around. In surgery you've got to be fast, focused, flexible — in my family, faithful. And it sure helps if you are a female. If you have these qualities it's going to work.

Hazel

Hazel believes that surgeons are born, not trained. Surgery is a talent, and the task of residency is really to develop the gift. Deciding to become a surgeon was not difficult for her. When she was growing up she was influenced by a neurosurgeon who had established a scholarship that allowed her to go to college, and consequently she wanted to become a neurosurgeon. But her exposure to general surgery changed that.

> I just walked in the operating room one day and I decided that was what I really wanted to do. I remember the first day I went in the operating room. They were doing a hernia case. I said, "This is what I want to do." And from that time, that is what I've wanted to do and I've pursued it.

The journey of developing her surgical skills was not always an easy one for Hazel, but after her graduation from medical school in 1992, she pursued her goal to the end. She tends to downplay the difficulties of her residency.

> In general it turned out to be a pretty good experience, as far as surgery residencies went. I compared it to some of my other friends that I met later, other women surgeons, a couple of them Black, but most of them White, and they had experiences that were far more difficult than mine.

Her way of coping with the tremendous demands of residency was to insist on enjoying other activities.

> Some of the advice that I was given as I was trying to decide to go into surgery was that I would have no life. I wouldn't be able to do this, I wouldn't be able

to do that. I wouldn't be able to go anywhere or do anything. Well, when I was a resident I went everywhere and I did everything! I think that you have to be organized, but it can be a really good experience as long as you realize that nothing is forever. Even when you're going through something difficult, it's not forever and there is always a light at the end of the tunnel. The thing you have to do is to make time to have a life. You have to do that. Even when I was tired, if my friends said, "Let's go somewhere," especially if it was people outside of the hospital, I did it. My philosophy was that if I can stay up all night working, I can stay up all night having fun. Things that I enjoyed doing I made time to do. I wasn't able to do them as often, but I made time to do them.

One of the reasons Hazel selected her residency program was that a relatively large number of women were either in the program at the time or had finished the program. Yet, she knew of instances where women were treated differently than their male colleagues. She describes it as not being overt or overwhelming but present, and if she didn't experience it herself, she was aware of it happening to other women residents.

I did have problems with one particular junior resident and I think that the way that it was handled by the whole surgical education board was indicative of the fact that I was a woman and I was criticizing someone who they thought was a good resident. He was male. That was my only experience where I really felt that there was a difference between the way I was treated and the men.

But even in that, even though there was disagreement, I was quite surprised that they would take his side against mine, seeing that I was the most senior person...I had been there longer. There weren't many serious repercussions; for example, no one tried to make my life miserable.

Hazel describes relationships with attendings — all of whom, with one exception, were male — as having had a different character for the women residents than for the men. Many of the attendings had either been through the surgery residency at that institution, or had attended the university, gone to other institutions to do their residencies, and returned as attendings. They tended to be relatively young, and they formed casual relationships with the male residents through activities like basketball. This resulted in a camaraderie that the women did not experience.

Not having that camaraderie didn't make much difference in terms of my getting to do cases and things like that. But I think that it may have changed the experience when it came to some other things — for instance, who gets an award for the best resident of the year, and that sort of thing. When I looked at how some of those things were done, it was clear to me that those kinds of relationships played a role in things like that.

The one female attending in the residency program was not a role model for Hazel. To Hazel, she appeared to have been impacted by being a woman in that system.

She did advise me of one thing once, which was important. She said, "On rounds you should speak up more and you should quote literature and stuff, don't just read the stuff, but you need to quote it so people can know what you're thinking." And I remember her, particularly, telling me that and it did make a difference. But she was not someone that I looked up to and I think that also had to do with the system: the fact that the other attendings did not show her that sort of respect, and it led to the residents, both male and female, not showing her that sort of respect. Her skills were not the best — they weren't the worst — but they weren't the best, and she really was not someone that we looked up to. And part of it had to do with the fact that she was a woman, too, and the fact that it was generally known that her own colleagues didn't respect her, and it filtered down into us as residents, even us as female residents, to not respect her. Because for years I'd say, "Oh, we have no female attendings…oh, that's right…she's there." Which is unfortunate. It would have been nice if we had someone who was like the way my colleague and I are for the residents here. We're well respected and looked up to. The nursing staff in the ICU and the ER, time and time again have talked about the difference in this program since we've been here. Things like that just didn't happen. Her presence there was just not felt. Not by us as female residents or by the program itself.

If you're the only woman attending, unless you're a star…I mean, to be average and the only woman attending is difficult. And I think that was the case with her. I was surprised that she gave me that advice, because it would have been nice if she had taken it herself and had been more present there for us.

Despite the residency program being pyramidal, Hazel's experience was that all of the women who wanted to remain in the program did advance. There were at least two female residents in almost every level of the program, but the program had not really developed systems to support women residents. Hazel recounts another situation where her being female influenced her residency experience.

> There were two women in my year, and when the other woman got pregnant it kind of fell to me to take over some of her duties. I thought that was unfair. It should have been spread out more evenly. If they weren't going to send her to a particular rotation because of her pregnancy, I shouldn't have to be the one to have to do a second of any rotation because she was pregnant. And I felt that had to do with two things: number one, we were friends and so I suppose they assumed that because we were friends, you know, I should be the one covering for her, and I also think it's because I was the other woman in the program at that level.

There were other ways that women were treated differently.

> I thought that they were definitely overly critical of some women residents. Also there were some differences in how attitudes were seen, for example, if a female resident opposed somebody or was verbal or made a stink about something then she was labeled as having an attitude. As opposed to when the males did it. Then it was just thought that they were standing up for themselves, they were doing the right thing. So there were little subtle things like that, but nothing overt and nothing really abrasive.

Hazel did her residency at a predominantly Black institution and had few negative experiences that she attributed to race. As a medical student at a White university she felt that the scant support for her decision to become a surgeon was racially based.

> A lot of the faculty and so-called advisors told me that I should do something that was not so hard. But they really weren't concerned about my interests, they were just looking at a Black woman who wanted to do surgery, and they were in a program where they'd never finished a Black person, and had only finished one woman.

She does remember one episode from residency that she believes was largely about race.

> When I was chief resident and I was administrative chief, we all took turns in making up the schedule and doing other administrative functions. And, pretty much, everyone was allowed to make up whatever schedule they wanted to make up, and it was no problem. Until I made up a schedule and the one White guy in our program complained because he didn't like it. Well, the surgery administrator changed the schedule. And I just was so upset because I thought that was just absolute nonsense. That resident was going to get his turn. Then he could make up whatever schedule he wanted. I was given this position of administrative chief for this time, but because this one person complained the schedule had to be changed to suit him. I thought it was just totally inappropriate.

I think it had to do with many factors. First of all, I think he finished because he was the White guy in the program. Not that he couldn't make it, because, obviously, he finished and he passed his boards, but there were other people who got cut from the program who would have also been able to finish and do well. And they kept him in the program in spite of the fact that he also had a substance abuse problem. And for some reason, they bent over backwards to keep this guy in the program. I think it's a fault of us as minorities where we feel that we have to bend over backwards to be so fair to the others yet they don't take that time with us. They look for reasons to kick us out, we look for reasons to make sure that we're not being prejudiced. I know if it was the opposite situation and he was the one Black guy who was in a majority White program, he would have been out the door a long time ago. He finished and he's a surgeon, he's in the military and that's fine, but that experience has always bothered me. That was not a female issue. That was just a plain old White issue and a slave mentality which we can never seem to get away from. I do believe that that was not really a female issue, that was definitely a race thing.

Another experience of residency is learning to deal with the inevitable patient deaths and difficult communications with families. Hazel's residency program provided no help in learning how to cope with these situations — either professionally or personally.

We had no guidance. We had absolutely none. I drew on my Christian experience, which I still do, in terms of being able to deal with situations like that. Especially situations with children or when there is a patient who you work with for months in the ICU and initially there was hope, and then it was gone until finally they expired — and you had to deal with that. There were no sessions, nothing to help anyone to deal with it. I just drew on my own Christian experience to help me to deal with it, but there was nothing there available for that.

I remember the first time someone died that I tried to save. You remember things like that. And how you tried to deal with it. And some of the residents didn't deal with it very well. Often if you had a bad day the response was, "Oh, let's all go out and get a drink." That is not necessarily the best way to deal with it — not that the residents were drunks. But that was the way, you know, if something happened, "Let's go out and get a drink and have a good time and forget about it."

But it's not really dealing with it. And I think what some of us did was to distance ourselves from the patients. You know, you treat them as a case, the aorta, the gallbladder, the spleen, so that it's not the patient, but the case. It happened a lot. In fact, there was one point in time when one of the attendings actually talked about it in Grand Rounds. That we should not be referring to patients as "the breast cancer," or whatever. That we should refer to them as patients, because, I guess, they had noticed it on rounds. But they didn't talk about how to deal with the emotion of seeing them as patients.

The extent to which coping with difficulty was expected was demonstrated by a story Hazel related about one of the other female residents.

> There are times when I thought that the women were being more criticized, or more easily criticized than the men. I remember Dr. X who was a couple of years ahead of me. She received a lot of criticism, even from her peers, that I thought was unwarranted. But she passed her Boards and I'm very happy for that. I thought that they were overly critical of her during a difficult period of her residency. Her father was also a physician and, unfortunately, he actually died in the middle of her surgery residency, and for part of the time she was the doctor taking care of him. We all took care of him. He had cancer.
>
> It was really hard and people were sympathetic to her on the surface, but in the reality of it, it was like, "Oh yeah, we're sorry about your father but, you know, you should be carrying your own weight. You should be doing this or that." In retrospect, it may have been better for her if she had taken leave, but she didn't. But even so, I still thought that they were overly critical of her.

When she first decided to become a surgeon, Hazel's friends worried that going into surgery would change her from the nice person she had been into someone who was mean and terrible. She is aware of being changed by the experience but in ways that she feels have been good for her.

> I see some differences but I think that they're positive differences. Even though I wanted to be a surgeon, in

many ways I was always accommodating towards people. For example, if somebody needed to change their schedule because they had something to do, I would always change with them. I was always much more accommodating. Now I think of myself more, and even so, I'm not nearly as selfish as I need to be. But, I think surgery residency has taught me some of those things, which even though they may seem to be negative on the surface, like being more selfish, are definitely more positive. They are things that I need in order to survive — not just residency but life in general, especially life in the surgical field. If you continue to accommodate others you can accommodate yourself out of it.

I'm definitely more vocal, not that I was real quiet back then, but I'm definitely more vocal. I will state my opinion even when it might put my career at risk, whereas that's not something that I would have done before. I would think about it, but I wouldn't say anything. Now I'll say what's on my mind, what I think of the situation. So, even though they may seem to be negative characteristics, for me, I think that they actually helped me. Also, I'm less tolerant of what I call foolishness in certain behavior, whereas before residency I was definitely more tolerant.

Another change that came a little later was the development of empathy.

Probably we surgeons should be more empathetic towards life, towards people, but I think we fall into the role of being less so, just because of the nature of what we do and also because of the fact that we're so busy that we don't have that much time to sit and reflect and think about some of the other aspects in life. What I have found, what I have come to realize, is that during residency you're very work oriented and everything is work to finish, work to do. Whatever you need to do is kind of work oriented. But as an attending, I've had more time to focus not just on doing the work — drawing the blood, doing the labs, doing the surgery — but on how the patient is dealing with the loss of her breast. Even as a woman, I don't think I was very empathetic towards these women during residency. You know, it was, "It needs to come off," or you do a lumpectomy, or whatever. But just the thought of someone's cutting into someone else's breast didn't really start to dawn on me, I think, until near the end of my residency. And one of the things that brought it forward was that one of our female attendings died from breast cancer. And the wife of another attending had breast cancer. And they were both young women — meaning forty or less. And that is when I really started thinking. Because now you actually know somebody. But during medical school and even during residency, when we first started talking about doing lumpectomy, I was like, "No, it has to come off." But you don't think of the whole person and how it's affecting them.

One of Hazel's best memories is of an encounter with a patient whom she had treated for a relatively simple surgical condition. It was a situation where she became aware of the impact that she had on the life of another woman.

I can think of one particular experience that I'll always remember. I took care of a young lady who had something real simple. I think it was a benign breast mass or something like that. She had children. And she was just so excited that I was taking care of her and she told me she wished that her children had role models that they could follow to know that they don't have to go — even on the pathway where she went — that there's another way in which you could live your life.

In summing up her residency experience Hazel describes it as a journey.

I would have to say that it was probably like going on a jungle trip. Even though I've never done one, I imagine it's like going through the Amazon jungle or the jungle in Zaire. It's very difficult and there are a lot of things that you have to go through. But when you get to where you want to go and you see the beautiful scenery, you know you'd never appreciate it as much unless you actually see it there. Or you see some wildlife that no matter how much you see it on TV you wouldn't appreciate it until you actually see it in person.

It was still worth it, but you're definitely going to come out with some bug bites and some scratches, and people can lose their lives along the way. You have to be well prepared going in. Because if you're not, the elements would eat you alive. At the end you have a tremendous feeling of accomplishment.

Xena

I had a break in my residency when I worked off my student loans. After doing two years at hospital A, I did my loan payback job and then I still ended up spending four years in my second program at hospital B, finishing in 1991. At the beginning I thought, "Yeah, I'm gonna do this. This is gonna be good." Then, while I was at A I thought, "I'm gonna do this, and this is gonna be hard." I felt like I lost part of myself during that second year at A, and I felt broken when I left there. After working I felt like I got some of myself back.

While doing the loan payback, I got over being sleep deprived, slowed my pace of life down, and felt like I'd regained some of myself. That was a good time for me, and when I left there and went back into residency, I went broad-shouldered. Sort of like twelve-year-old girls before they lose it all. And it was like: "I am Odysseus. You cannot stop me. I have this knowledge. I'm going to go forth. And I'm going to finish. This is my journey."

In my first six months at B I was vocal. I said what I thought, I had opinions about things, and I spent that first six months getting my face bloody. And it wasn't a slap, I mean, it was bloody, and they hit me until I couldn't get up anymore!

Then I got quiet. I said "OK, I will have these same opinions, but I will not express them." And then they found anything they could to beat me up again about. I knew that every holiday I would be on call and every complication would be put under a microscope. About halfway through I was starting to feel not only broken but not even repairable. And by the time I finished, I felt like, "I'll finish this, but whether or not I want to do this, I'm not sure, because of what it has done to me." I felt like a third of a person. I felt like I would have to spend a lot of time post-residency learning how to be a person again. But it didn't feel like it felt when I left the first place. It didn't feel like losing myself, it felt like I'd been disembodied, ravaged, and I had to think long and hard about whether or not I wanted to do this, and if I did it, how I would choose to do it. I felt definitely changed, and the only thing I could do was look back and say "Well, I did this despite you." But I'm not as happy with the outcome as I thought I would be and I'm not even sure it was worth it.

Xena's residency experience is a story of pain and triumph. She had the unusual experience of interrupting her training for three years to fulfill a loan obligation remaining from medical school. She credits this break with reawakening her and keeping her close to her experience. As a consequence, she remained aware of just how dehumanizing surgical training was for her and how important it was for her to be aware of her feelings.

I think surgeons are people that actually start out very caring, but because of the nature of what we do we put that caring away so that we can do what we need to do. And some surgeons can't pull that back out. As a whole, I think the training programs dehumanized you. I think I've worked hard to not be that way and to stay close to my experience.

Key to Xena's experience was the amount of pain she has felt and continues to feel about her residency. She feels that being a Black female compounded the pain and difficulties of residency. And the triumph of the experience was how she not only finished but used reserves of strength to survive and grow from the experience.

Xena's family members, medical professionals themselves, were not supportive of her decision to attend medical school or, after graduation, to become a surgeon.

> My own blood family, other than some distant cousins, never offered me any support. My uncle, a neurologist in an academic environment, said to my father, "She'll never make it.' My parents, my uncle, all said, "I don't know why you did that, it was really stupid. I don't know why you decided to be a surgeon. You should have been a pediatrician. You should have been a teacher."

Encounters with other medical personnel and patients compounded Xena's experiences of isolation and lack of support. She recalls several incidents where patients and attendings would express doubt that she was really a surgeon.

> Many patients would say, "Well, I never had a girl doctor, never had a girl surgeon." And even though your white coat says surgeon, people would still ask, "Does that mean you're learning to be a surgeon?" They had a hard time with that. And still today, usually I walk in the room with a white coat on and a name tag, and oftentimes I am asked to empty the trash or the bedpan.

Xena believes that her experiences differed from those of her male peers in many ways: in the informal coaching attending surgeons gave preferentially to the male residents, in the reluctance of attendings to allow Xena to perform parts of operations, and in the overt comments of physicians in positions of power.

> My program director said, "We let girls into the program because we think they're cute, and then by the time they get to be third- and fourth-years, we wonder if they know anything." That is a direct quote, I never forgot that, because I thought, Well, I thought I got into this program because I was qualified.

Living in this environment required a delicate dance.

> You're not getting the same coaching as the male residents. If you're aggressive, I mean if you act in a manner like guys do to get cases, then you're overly aggressive, it's that Catch 22. You're either a psychobitch or you're passive. And it takes about three or four years in a training program to figure out where the balance is so that you can at least be seen by others as not being too passive and not being an aggressive, hostile, psycho-bitch.

One experience that Xena remembers well involved the discounting of a Black female surgeon presenting at a national surgical meeting.

> She did a poster session but she also had about a twenty-minute presentation. At this point she had already passed her boards. I was standing right next to her and some guy said, "Doctor, huh? M.D.?" "Yes." "Are you a surgeon?" "Yes." "Board certified?" "Yes." "Really?"

As a Black female surgical resident, Xena felt that she needed to be on top of everything and could count on no one. Even as a chief resident it was difficult to delegate responsibilities to junior residents because if they were insubordinate she could not count on being supported by the system. Xena also experienced double standards in how surgical complications were reviewed. "If I had a complication in residency, I was always the example. But if somebody else had a complication who had skin of a different color or different gonads it was the exception."

But even being compulsively on top of things could have its drawbacks. Xena recounts the consequences of finding and asking about a patient's pathology report which suggested that the program director, who was the attending surgeon, possibly should have done more testing, or performed another operation.

> It wasn't pleasant to have the program chief call you into his office once a week and say, "I'm not gonna let you finish this program. If I have to fire you, I will write you a letter of recommendation to go to any program in the world, and anything except surgery. You can be [in] anesthesia, you can be [in] internal medicine, you can be a cardiologist." He said, "I will write you an excellent letter of recommendation, I don't think you're stupid." And then I said, "Well no, you know, gee, I want to be a surgeon," and so when that didn't work, then he started telling me I was stupid and I would never be able to be a surgeon. He said, "You're stupid. You'll never pass your boards." And of course, here I am struggling to pass my boards, and I don't hear his voice but for a while there wasn't a day that went by that I didn't hear his voice saying "You'll never pass your boards."

There were few other women residents and fewer Black women in Xena's residencies. Relationships between the women were often problematic because of the extreme fatigue, competitiveness, focus on finishing, and personality clashes. There were few or no female attendings who could act as role models. Xena characterizes many of the women surgeons she encountered as either having relinquished their female identities to become one of the guys, acting overly feminine to make sure that they don't get mistaken for one of the guys, or fighting to maintain their wholeness. The women surgeons she encountered were often discounted by their peers and treated disrespectfully.

In this environment, Xena had difficulty finding a way to be whole and still be a surgeon.

> I think the hardest task was trying to find a place where I thought I could see myself or see myself in. I didn't really find that in my internship year nor in my second year. I kept looking at these faces that I couldn't really relate to and couldn't really relate to me and didn't know what to do...other than have this stiff, sort of, intercourse about patients and, "Are you happy?"

> Initially, having a Black woman as chief surgical resident was one of the things that made me go to my second program. When I saw her, I thought, This will be great! I looked forward to it because I thought, Well, she's someone that's worked all the way through the system and might be able to give me some pointers. But none of that worked. And part of that might have been our personalities. So the only thing it did for me was...when you need to see your face somewhere.

I would say residency was hard. I think it was more difficult because of the color of my skin and that relates to not having someone that I could identify with. They don't have to be your friend, but someone you can identify with so that you can make some connection and say, OK, well, this is how this works.

You're always second-guessing yourself, because you never see your face on the other side. I think the ability to see yourself there as a woman — as an African American woman — not feel like you're going to be dodging bullets, would make it a lot better.

I think that in the world, as human beings, we ask ourselves, "What is our purpose?" and you look to see yourself someplace. And you may not look just to see your reflection, but you say, "If this is something I *want,* I can *do* this." And there's a message that comes to you in surgery: "Don't count on it."

Xena had the ability to finish her residency, reflect back on it, and use that experience to inform how she is in the world. Throughout her residency she had mini-triumphs that allowed her to keep on pursuing her goal of completion.

She took care of herself by buying "treats" for herself, taking vacations out of the area, having "lots of sex," and being in therapy. Xena built herself a support system. "I think it helped that I could always stay connected to someone so that when I was looking at it and I couldn't see light at the end of the tunnel…it was nice to have someone there that I could express those bare-bones thoughts to. Not anyone in the residency, but a partner."

She sees the residency training as an experience that had a deep impact on who she is as a person today. Xena describes the changes that resulted from her residency experience:

> The way I relate to human pain is different, because I think I have personal experience with it in a way that men and White females in that program can't relate to. I think it's a real up-front, personal, close feeling. I think that no one would ever describe me as a cocky person. I think that I maybe had that ability until residency, and I don't feel proud about it. You see these people that finish their training at places like the Mayo Clinic and they just think that they are fabulous, wonderful. I can't have that. People say, "No one can take your self-esteem away from you. No one can take your confidence away from you." But I think if you talk to people where there's been a concentrated effort to do that, which part of residency is...I don't want to glorify this, or sound histrionic about it, but I think it's sort of like talking to someone that was in a concentration camp. I wonder if they ever have that ability to be cocky again, and to regain their human dignity. You can't take that away from somebody, but something happens to it. It's different.

Xena believes the circumstances of her residency have, in some respects, resulted in her being a better surgeon.

> I hated being a resident and the only thing I can say it did do for me was, because I didn't have any privileges, and because I couldn't get away with anything — in the world, I feel more prepared than any of my colleagues. I've seen stuff that they have never seen and had to take care of and have had to make it work. And that's the good part about it.

The resolution comes with the ability to look back and make meaning of the experience.

> There's no way to make sense about it and make yourself think it was OK, 'cause it wasn't OK. The OK part about it is that you got out of it what you were supposed to and that was through your own working hard, and maybe there's some miracle involved in that as well.

Xena finds that the triumph comes with the finishing, and the feeling, and the understanding, and the integrating, and the continual striving to be whole.

> When I tell myself the story of my residency, I tell myself something that will make me feel good about it. I tell myself that I've been purified by the fire. And that, if I'm honest I know that a lot of the parts, a lot of the pain of it, wasn't necessary. There were some good parts. There were days when I actually could laugh and there were days when I had some clarity that, even though I was tired and angry, there was a patient in front of me and I could say to myself, "That's my problem. This person is here and they came here because they want me to help them. And that's my job. None of this other stuff matters." And I think that one of the things that I've done consistently is...the more painful it is, the more involved I'll be with patients, because that offsets the pain.

Chapter 5

Understanding the Residency Experience

Surgeons must be very careful
When they take the knife!
Underneath their fine incisions
Stirs the Culprit — Life!

~ Emily Dickinson

I used the stories of Diane, Janice, Joyce, Marie, Hazel, and Xena to tease out some of the essences of their residency experiences. I defined four facets of those experiences, which I have labeled *immersion, distancing, surfacing,* and *transcendence.* These are not linear stages, but rather aspects of experience.

Immersion

The life of a surgery resident is dominated by the pressures of never-ending work. Residents are totally immersed in the work to be done and the need to do this work flawlessly.

The day usually starts at about 5:00 a.m. with morning rounds. All hospitalized patients must be examined, their charts reviewed for changes since the last visit, new laboratory results analyzed, and the patients' vital information — weight, temperature, blood pressure, pulse, respirations — checked. If there are patients scheduled for surgery that day, everything must be reviewed to be sure that they are ready for the operations — all lab results accounted for, pre-operative preparations completed, consent forms signed, questions answered, etc.

It is the responsibility of the residents to be familiar with every detail of every patient on their service. They must know the patient's history, current status, and treatment plan. They must know the results of completed tests and when pending tests are scheduled. They must be familiar with the patient's symptoms, differential diagnosis, illness, surgical procedure, medications, and expected course. They must always be prepared to present this information to the surgeon in charge (the attending) and answer any questions the attending may have.

After rounds there may be surgery to assist with or to perform, lectures to attend, patients to see in the clinic or office, dressings to change or tubes to place. If the resident or team is "on call," they are responsible for all new admissions, consultations and emergencies for a stated period of time — usually in addition to their regular duties.

Call schedules vary. The most demanding is being on call every other day — working from 5:00 a.m. on day one until about 7:00 p.m. (or whenever the work is completed) on day two, then going home for a few hours of life and sleep until reporting for work and call on day three. This schedule, a standard in years past, is not routinely used currently but may occur when vacation schedules result in a shortage of residents. As a member of a trauma team, I worked "24 on, 24 off." We worked from 7:00 a.m. on day one until 7:00 a.m. on day two and then had 24 hours off. More commonly residents take call every three to four nights and every other or third weekend. Fifth- or sixth-year residents may be able to take call from home but must be able to get to the hospital immediately if needed. They will routinely carry pagers at all times to be available for their junior residents and the patients on their service. Residents are expected to rise above fatigue to meet the demands of patient care.

Several years ago a well publicized patient death in New York City was linked to resident inexperience and fatigue. As a result of this episode, the Libby Zion case, restrictions were placed on the hours that residents could work. For surgical residents, the outcome was a mandate that residents now have at least one 24-hour period per week with no involvement in patient care.

This pace of life allows no time for reflection or even for awareness of one's experiences.

> When things got rough I dealt with it by just working harder. (Marie)

> It was not too hard to bury [difficult experiences] because you're so busy. You're here talking to this family that somebody's dead and they're screaming and your beeper is going off and there is another crisis somewhere else that you need to attend to. I think there are a lot of unresolved crises inside of me. You just move on to the next one and then you've been up a day and a half and you fall asleep dead at the first opportunity. You don't even have time to think about it. It just ends up being swept away in the hustle. (Joyce)

I put everything on hold during residency. So even though you're up all night and you don't go home for Christmas, and you take call on New Year's, and you've got to work on Thanksgiving — those things were just a part of it. (Janice)

We're so busy that we don't have that much time to sit and reflect and think about some of the other aspects of life. During residency you're very work oriented and everything is work to finish, work to do. Whatever you need to do is kind of work oriented. But as an attending, I've had more time to focus not just on doing the work — drawing the blood, doing the labs, doing the surgery — but on how the patient is dealing with the loss of her breast. (Hazel)

I have labeled this state of being *immersion*. It is characterized by complete focus on the work at hand for long periods of time under stressful and fatiguing conditions. Any breaks from work are utilized for sleep or recreation, precluding awareness, reflection, examination and integration of experiences. This state of being was taken for granted by the physicians interviewed. They often saw it as a necessary means to a desired end, the price that had to be paid.

Medical students have an introduction to this total involvement in work, but without the responsibility held by residents. Immersion begins with the first day of residency and continues largely unabated until the senior year or years. There may be brief periods of less rigorous schedules if the resident has an opportunity to do elective rotations, and on the two weeks of vacation granted each year.

Even in the midst of this state of immersion there is for these Black women a nascent awareness of being different from their fellow residents, receiving different treatment, and needing to develop different survival strategies. Because they are being so immersed, and also because they rely on distancing, as discussed below, this awareness usually manifests itself in almost intuitive protective strategies — like playing down one's femaleness — rather than in active analysis of the situations, or in proactive challenges.

Distancing

The stressful nature of medical training has been written about in both the popular and academic literature. The impact of this environment on the development of empathy has been discussed by Mizrahi, and the risk of burnout for individuals in helping professions has been documented by Cherniss.[1]

A corollary of immersion is distancing — denial, or emotional blocking. This is the process by which residents separate themselves from their own emotional experiences. There is little in the medical literature on the coping mechanisms utilized by residents in dealing with their daily experiences. Mizrahi discussed the techniques internal medicine residents use to distance themselves from patients physically and psychologically.

> House officers got rid of patients physically by transferring, discharging, and at times refusing to receive them and by passing many responsibilities toward them down the medical hierarchy or across to social workers and other nonmedical staff. They distanced themselves from patients psychologically by adopting the mechanisms of omission, avoidance, and objectification.[2]

But Mizrahi did not consider those coping mechanisms that allow residents to distance themselves from their own emotional experiences.

Psychological terms for emotional distancing are *denial, repression,* or *dissociation.* The psychological literature views dissociative reactions as a means by which an individual avoids anxiety by "blocking out parts of his life or aspects of her personality.[3] This blocking out has been regarded by some as a maladaptive response or a symptom of pathology, but more commonly has come to be understood as an adaptive mechanism that may at times become pathological. Meichenbaum wrote: "In some stressful situations the most effective means of coping may be not engaging in reality testing or problem solving, but instead using some form of denial."[4] Bromberg quoted Putnam in calling dissociation "the escape when there is no escape." He went on to describe dissociation:

> As a global defense against ongoing trauma or the fear of potential trauma, it represents an adaptive hypnoidal capacity of the personality. It serves to protect against what Reik called shock: the real or perceived threat of being overwhelmingly incapacitated by aspects of reality that cannot be processed by existing cognitive schemata without doing violence to one's experience of selfhood and sometimes to sanity itself.[5]

Bromberg also said of dissociation:

> It is a basic process that allows individual self-states to function optimally (not simply defensively) when full immersion in a single reality, a single strong affect, and a suspension of one's self-reflective capacity is exactly what is called for or wished for.[5]

Emotional distancing was described by Lazarus and Lazarus as a way to "remove ourselves emotionally from the distressing meanings of a situation." They gave as an example their response to television coverage of the Vietnam War. "We had become so inured to the sights of suffering that we were seeing without really seeing, having distanced ourselves from the emotional meanings of death and suffering."[6]

The early literature on post-traumatic stress disorders (PTSD) gives brief mention of dissociation or "psychic numbing" as a coping mechanism which, when combined with other diagnostic criteria, is characteristic of PTSD.[7] More recently, Janoff-Bulman provided a more thorough discussion of mechanisms used to cope with traumatic events.

> Two seemingly contradictory sets of processes constitute the primary psychological responses to traumatic life events. One set, characterized by denial and emotional numbing, represents efforts to avoid painful thoughts, images, and feelings. A second set, characterized by intrusions and re-experiencing of the trauma, represent efforts to confront them. Victims alternate between the need to approach the trauma and to avoid it, to confront their experience and protect themselves from it....
>
> Unfortunately, in considering denial and intrusive recollections as indicative of trauma, we have too often considered them abnormal responses to stressful events, rather than adaptive responses to abnormal events.... We have over-pathologized denial and intrusion as problematic symptoms and have too often failed to recognize their considerable adaptive value.[8]

Janoff-Bulman discussed denial as behavior that individuals use to protect themselves acutely at the time of the event, and to maximize the possibility of eventually integrating the experience. "Denial processes are 'chosen' as an automatic response to overpowering new data.... It is the process of denial that prevents a steady, unmodulated attack in the victim's cognitive-emotional world. Denial enables the survivor to more gradually face the realities of the victimization and incorporate the experience into his or her internal world." Janoff-Bulman defined two aspects of denial:

> ...one involving thoughts and ideas related to the victimization, the other involving feelings and emotions. The "turning off" of cognition has more generally been discussed in terms of denial and the "turning off" of emotions has generally been discussed in terms of numbing, particularly psychic numbing or emotional anesthesia.

> In order to minimize the threat posed by the traumatic event, the victim typically disavows information and feels little or nothing in response to this information. The initial onslaught is so massive, the cognitive upheaval and emotional responses (e.g., fear and anxiety) so intense, that the cognitive-emotional system largely shuts down; denial processes are invoked, and the victim acknowledges and feels little.[8]

While there are clear differences between the experiences of surgical residents and trauma victims — perhaps most significantly, the power associated with being a physician — there are important overlaps. Surgical residents are barraged by unfamiliar events often involving physical and emotional discomfort for patients. Residents perform a number of procedures, often painful, on patients in the context of learning skills and providing treatment. Residents are immersed in an unremittingly high-stress environment, and the stress is exacerbated by uncertainty about their own capabilities, expectations of perfection, fatigue, and overwork. They have no control over their schedules or their workload. They are expected to deal with emotionally overwhelming situations — informing family members of the death of a loved one; treating trauma victims in the emergency department — with little prior training, no discussion of the emotional impact, and no opportunity to debrief afterwards. In such situations, where there is no opportunity to process the personal impact of events, emotional numbing is a valuable coping mechanism.

That they used distancing, denial, dissociation, and repression as coping mechanisms, both personally and in dealing with patients, was evident in the comments of the women interviewed.

> If a patient had a long and lingering illness you might have them on your service for a long period of time and end up interacting with the family a lot. Then you could see the residents trying to withdraw. You could tell it was a drain emotionally on them but it was very much an unaddressed set of issues. (Diane)

> We had no guidance [in dealing with emotionally difficult situations]. We had absolutely none. I drew on my Christian experience, which I still do in terms of being able to deal with situations like that. Often if you had a bad day the response was, "Oh, let's all go out and get a drink and forget about it." And I think what some of us did was to distance ourselves from the patients. You treat them as a case, the aorta, the gallbladder, the spleen, so that it's not the patient but the case. (Hazel)

> When I was a resident I didn't have the human side. That was pushed back. (Janice)

> I think surgeons are people that actually start out very caring but because of the nature of what we do we put that caring away so that we can do what we need to do. And some surgeons can't pull that back out. As a whole, I think the training programs dehumanized you. I think I've worked hard to not be that way and to stay close to my experience. (Xena)

> I think I buried all that (the difficult emotional experiences). It wasn't too hard to bury because you're so busy. You don't even have time to think about it. It just ends up being swept away in the hustle. (Joyce)

The characteristics of immersion and distancing are likely to be congruent with the experiences of most, if not all, surgical residents. What then is distinct about the experiences of Black women surgical residents?

That women of color in the United States are significantly impacted by racism and sexism, both individual and institutionalized, is generally accepted knowledge.[9] This was succinctly stated by McGoldrick, Garcia-Preto, Moore Hines, & Lee. "Even professional Black women do not escape the effects of racism and sexism; they encounter frequent clinical dilemmas because they do not meet the image their clients expect, namely a White male."[10] Essed discussed "gendered racism" experienced by professional Black women.

> On a macro-societal level, [gendered] racism operates through various mechanisms. Black women are (a) marginalized, (b) culturally problematized, and (c) impaired in social mobility. They encounter paternalism, they are underestimated, their work is ethnicized, and they generally have fewer career opportunities than men and White women, respectively. These mechanisms operate simultaneously and probably stimulate each other.[11]

While many of the comments made by the Black women surgeons in my study reflect experiences of gendered racism as described by Essed, and the experiences of tokens as described by Rosabeth Moss Kanter, it is noteworthy that the majority of women interviewed minimized their experiences of racism and sexism. Hooks discussed repression of feelings as a survival tactic for Black people that may have begun in slavery.

> The practice of repressing feelings as a survival strategy continued to be an aspect of Black life long after slavery ended.... In the world view of many Black people, it became a positive attribute to be able to contain feelings. Over time, the ability to mask, hide, and contain feelings came to be viewed by many Black people as a sign of strong character.[12]

In the intense residency environment it is easy for one to be unaware of one's surroundings and of one's own experiences. The coping mechanisms of distancing and denial used in dealing with difficult clinical experiences appeared also to be utilized to deal with personal experiences of being treated differently. This was facilitated by being immersed in the work.

> There probably was [racism and sexism] but I was so focused on doing what I felt needed to be done. (Marie)

> If I was treated differently I didn't notice. I notice being treated differently a lot more now that I've been out of residency. It's a lot more obvious. I look back and I think it must have happened in residency too, and I just didn't pick up on it or I kept it at a subconscious level and didn't react to it. (Joyce)

> You can see the pattern [of gender inequality] now.
> It's hard when you're in it, to know whether it's you,
> or is it because you're female or is it something else?
> It's hard to sort that stuff out when you're in the
> middle of it, but when you sit back you know that
> you've been there and you've seen that as a resident
> and it comes out more clearly. (Janice)

When these women did become aware of differential treatment during their residencies, it became an additional burden
that they had to shoulder, a burden that their male colleagues
didn't face. Immersion and distancing served to push these
awarenesses aside.

> In my first six months in my second program, I was
> vocal. I said what I thought, I had opinions about
> things, and I spent that first six months getting my
> face bloody. (Xena)

> I had a lot of problems the first couple of years. One
> of the big problems was the fact that I was a female
> and then that I was Black. There are stories that go
> on and on about, 'Your doctor is not only Black, she's
> female...your doctor is not only female, she's Black.'
> (Marie)

> The reason why I always wear a T-shirt under my
> scrubs is because scrubs are not cut for women, and
> so when you lean forward...men used to...you could
> tell they were looking down your shirt. It happened
> all the time. You can't bend over and take care of the
> patient who's bleeding on the floor without worrying
> about somebody looking down your shirt. The male
> residents didn't have to deal with that. (Janice)

I really tried to minimize my femaleness. I never wore pastel colors and never wore my hair out.... I wanted people to look at me as a doctor and a surgeon and not a woman who is a surgeon. (Janice)

Even though there were several women that finished before me, there is still such a long-standing, ingrained sense that surgery is a field for men. The women were not treated overtly differently but that attitude was always there.... There was also a tendency to lump all the women together. (Diane)

Some of the women interviewed acknowledged the difficulty of knowing whether the treatment they experienced during residency was related to race or gender. "You can see the pattern now. It's hard when you're in it to know whether it's you, or is it because you're female or is it something else?" (Janice)

Most, however, felt that in the strongly male-dominated field of surgery, gender was more significant than race.

There were a couple of Black men that were in the program for several years before leaving for other programs and I didn't get the sense that they were having as much resistance from the attendings about giving up cases. When I compared my experiences with the White women in the program they seemed to have the same complaint as I. (Diane)

Because of the dearth of Black males in most residency programs, having a Black male to compare experiences with was uncommon.

Surfacing

During senior residency or after residency, the pace of life slowed for the women interviewed and they had time to take in their surroundings, experiences, and emotions. They had more time for relationships. And they had time to reflect on these experiences and awarenesses and begin to integrate them. This was reflected in their comments.

> So it's kind of retrospective. Now that I have those things [family, husband, other concerns] my perspective is very different. (Janice)

> We see stuff here [at my current attending position] all the time. There's no question that it's sexist. [Female residents] are berated more on rounds, given more scut to do. You can see the pattern now. (Janice)

> As an attending, I've had more time to focus not just on doing the work, but on how the patient is dealing with the loss of her breast. (Hazel)

> Even as a woman, I don't think I was very empathetic towards [women with breast cancer] during residency. But just the thought of someone's cutting into someone else's breast didn't really start to dawn on me until near the end of my residency. And one of the things that brought it forward was that one of our female attendings died from breast cancer. And that is when I really started thinking. Because now you actually know somebody. (Diane)

> I notice being treated differently a lot more now that I've been out of residency. I look back and I think it must have happened in residency too and I just didn't pick up on it or I kept it at a subconscious level and didn't react to it. (Joyce)

> Now that I look back at it there were people that were difficult individuals, residents and attendings. There were attendings that may have used personality things to disguise racism. During my residency I did not feel...but maybe I would not allow myself to feel. (Marie)

This change in perspective is also reflected in some of the metaphors they used to describe their residency experiences.

> It's like you're submerged for a long period of time trying to get some particular goal or prize and then you finally get to come up for air. (Diane)

> It was like going on a jungle trip. It's very difficult and there are a lot of things that you have to go through. But when you get to where you want to go and you see the beautiful scenery, you know you'd never appreciate it as much unless you actually see it there. (Hazel)

Ongoing daily exposure to the racism and sexism that is the norm in American life may have been instrumental for these women in their coming to awareness. Decreased pace of life, altered responsibilities, and increased reflective time allowed them to open to the recognition of the emotional impact of their patient experiences and the episodes of racism and sexism in their present lives.

Surfacing from the all-consuming period of residency presents opportunities to begin to experience and understand what it means to be a Black female surgeon in the United States. On reflection, some experienced themselves as changed, others as essentially the same.

> I see some differences, but I think that they're positive differences.... I was always much more accommodating. Now I think of myself more...I'm definitely more

> vocal. I will state my opinion even when it might put my career at risk, whereas that's not something that I would have done before. (Hazel)

> [Residency] made me a better doctor...but it also made me a different person because it allowed me really to appreciate the life part of it. We see suffering and pain and people dying all the time, and when you really take it into the context that it should be...of where your life is...that makes it different. After I finished my training I realized that there were things that I just would not compromise. I think that the whole experience ends up making you a different person. For the women, I think it makes us better in that it allows us to help people coming behind us. (Janice)

In this research, Xena is the one woman who had a different experience and may be seen as the exception that proves the rule. Although she, like the others, was immersed in her residency, she had a hiatus of three years in her training. It was this interruption that gave her time to reflect and limited her ability to utilize distancing on her return to training. "At the loan payback job I got over being sleep deprived, slowed my pace of life down, and felt like I'd regained some of myself." On her return to residency she was acutely aware of being treated differently because she was a Black woman. Of all my interviewees, she was the most articulate about the pain she experienced during residency, pain that she attributes to racism and sexism.

> I knew that every holiday I would be on call and every complication would be put under a microscope... It didn't feel like losing myself, it felt like I'd been disembodied, ravaged.... You're not getting the same

coaching as the male residents. If you're aggressive — I mean if you act in a manner like guys do to get cases — then you're overly aggressive.... I would say residency was hard. I think it was more difficult because of the color of my skin and that relates to not having someone that I could identify with. (Xena)

Immersed in her residency but unable to distance herself from it, Xena coped by building herself a support system.

I think it helped that I could always stay connected to someone so that when I was looking at it and I couldn't see light at the end of the tunnel...it was nice to have someone there that I could express those bare-bones thoughts to. (Xena)

This type of connection most likely helped her to process the difficult experiences she encountered and make meaning of them. She also was able to use her suffering as a way of personal growth. Polly Young-Eisendrath wrote of suffering as "one of the engines of human development" and as instrumental in the development of compassion. "Compassion, the knowledge that comes from suffering with others, is a tremendous gift. It comes from deeply and truthfully recognizing your own suffering and pain, valuing it for its truth, its thereness."[13] Xena finds similar meaning in her experiences of suffering.

The way I relate to human pain is different because I think I have personal experience with it in a way that men and White females in that program can't relate to. When I tell myself the story of my residency, I tell myself something that will make me feel good about it. I tell myself that I've been purified by the fire. (Xena)

It is in the process of surfacing that the women interviewed begin to become more aware of their residency experiences, re-experience the suppressed emotions, and begin to integrate the experiences into their lives by making meaning of them. Part of this is a process of self-actualization and self-recovery, as described by hooks. "Many Black females have learned to deny our inner needs while we develop our capacity to cope and confront in public life."[12] It is a process of opening to experience and acknowledging individual needs and wants.

> Now I think of myself more, and even so, I'm not nearly as selfish as I need to be. (Hazel)

> After I finished my training I realized that there were things that I just would not compromise. That now that I've made it through there were things that I won't give up. Anything that has to do with my family comes first. So I guess it allowed me to realize what my priorities are. (Janice)

Transcendence

The women interviewed demonstrated a strong attraction to surgery and to their work with patients. This is what keeps them engaged in the long and arduous process.

> I always knew I was going to be a doctor and I always knew I was going to be a surgeon. (Marie)

> [Surgery] is such an emotional high. It's so ego gratifying when you feel like you've really done something. I guess when we come to medicine we all have whatever baggage we bring. We all do it for different reasons. And for me it was always about taking care of

patients and really...I don't know why I'm getting teary eyed, but it's very emotional. (Janice)

One of the things that I've done consistently is...the more painful it is, the more involved I'll be with patients, because that offsets the pain. (Xena)

I would never go back and undo it. I'm really glad I'm doing it. I think I did the right thing. I think it is what God intended me to do. It just feels right. (Joyce)

I just walked in the operating room one day and I decided that was what I really wanted to do. I remember the first day I went in the operating room. They were doing a hernia case. I said, "This is what I want to do." And from that time, that is what I've wanted to do, and I've pursued it. (Hazel)

The experiences these women have in surgery are similar to the peak experiences described by Maslow. O'Connell and O'Connell quoted Maslow's description of peak experiences:

Feelings of limitless horizons opening up to the vision, the feeling of being simultaneously more powerful and also more helpless than one ever was before, the feeling of great ecstasy and wonder and awe, the loss of placing in time and space with, finally, the conviction that something extremely important and valuable had happened, so that the subject is to some extent transformed and strengthened even in his daily life by such experiences.[14]

These women's experiences also embody the concept of flow, or optimal experience, as discussed by Csikszentmihalyi. He described these experiences as containing at least one and often all of eight major components.

First, the experience usually occurs when we confront tasks we have a chance of completing. Second, we must be able to concentrate on what we are doing. Third and fourth, the concentration is usually possible because the task undertaken has clear goals and provides immediate feedback. Fifth, one acts with a deep but effortless involvement that removes from awareness the worries and frustrations of everyday life. Sixth, enjoyable experiences allow people to exercise a sense of control over their actions. Seventh, concern for the self disappears, yet paradoxically the sense of self emerges stronger after the flow experience is over. Finally, the sense of the duration of time is altered; hours pass by in minutes, and minutes can stretch out to seem like hours. The combination of all these elements causes a sense of deep enjoyment that is so rewarding people feel that expending a great deal of energy is worthwhile simply to be able to feel it.[15]

I have chosen to call this state, as experienced by surgery residents (and practicing surgeons, in my personal experience), *transcendence*. It is an experience that lifts one out of one's daily routine into a state of timeless synergy. In the operating room the experience is that of being the lead in a coordinated and seamless dance. There is an economy of movement, a sharpening of attention, a focusing of awareness, and a sense of rightness and harmony. It is these occasional and enticing episodes of transcendence that provide the incentive to tolerate the more difficult residency experiences.

Relationship to the Literature

As discussed earlier, there is little in the literature about Black female physicians. Epps in discussing Black women in medicine expressed concern at the lack of Black female role models, and feared the disconnection of Black women physicians from support and social systems in the Black communities.[16] The women I interviewed confirmed the scarcity of Black female role models but were able to maintain ties with their families and communities. They were able to develop support systems that met their individual needs.

McNamara noted how frequently women decide not to enter surgery, despite preferring it. "Sixty-six percent of men who preferred surgery chose it while only thirty-one percent of women who preferred it pursued it as a career."[17] All of the women interviewed in this study said that they selected a surgical career because they enjoyed the practice of surgery. While McNamara believed that the choice of surgery is influenced by role model availability, the prevailing attitude of the profession, and training opportunities, these elements did not emerge as being instrumental for this group of women.

Some of the women interviewed, most notably Janice, used strategies similar to those reviewed by Ortiz in her look at the process of professional incorporation in residency for women. She presented the situation of a Dr. Masters. "Dr. Masters had to resolve the dilemma of being a woman in a man's world. The latter was accomplished by two concurrent strategies: overt denial of the feminine role and the maximization of the doctor role."[18] All of the women studied stressed the importance of the doctor role and many of them used their work with patients to ground themselves when residency became more difficult.

Kinder compared the differences between "early" women in surgery and current residents. Of the pioneers, she stated, "If we women reflected at all on the [long hours and sacrifice of a more balanced lifestyle], we concluded that total commitment was necessary in order to be an excellent surgeon." She described women entering surgical programs at the time the article was written as being less willing to compromise other life choices for a surgical career and as being outspoken about "what they believe are the inappropriate rigors of the traditional residency."[19] Although two of the women interviewed in my study entered residency in 1986 and 1987, they did not have the same freedom as the young women described by Kinder. Even the youngest members of the interview group had experiences similar to those of Kinder's pioneers.

My participants' experiences were similar to those of other Black women surgeons, as described by Sterling. Her interviewees saw gender as the salient element in their experiences of discrimination in residency.[20] To the extent that the women I interviewed were cognizant of their experiences in the moment, they noticed gender more often than race as being the relevant factor. This is consistent with surgery as one of the last bastions of male domination in medicine. In this setting it becomes easy to see how infiltration by women — of any race — represents such a significant threat to the status quo that race becomes secondary.

Summary

The women whom we have briefly met in this study are all unique individuals. I have not discussed their individual demographic characteristics, in order to maintain their anonymity. The cohort of Black women surgeons is so small — estimated at .0005% of all general surgeons by Numann (in Organ & Kosiba)[21] — that they could be easily identified by small defining characteristics. They share the common characteristics of being Black women surgeons who are roughly of the same generation. Their exposure to the dominant White culture in educational settings varies widely, with some spending much of their time in predominantly Black institutions and others having the opposite experiences. None of the six women had physician parents, although two had mothers who were nurses. They had few role models. They are true pioneers.

These surgeons' stories reflect the intensity of their feelings about the profession they have chosen and their willingness to undergo the bittersweet experiences of residency. Each woman's story contains many stories, and together they weave the pattern of surgical residency experiences for Black women general surgeons in all its diversity and complexity. The stories, by themselves, are significant in giving voice to previously unheard experiences of a traditionally silenced group. In this aspect they speak for themselves.

Taken as a whole, the stories shed new light on the states of immersion, distancing, surfacing, and transcendence in the residency experiences of Black female general surgeons. They provide new insight into the depth and intensity of the experience.

Chapter 6

Research Influences and Process

This research is a qualitative study of practicing Black women surgeons. I elected to use qualitative methods for this research because they were the most appropriate means of answering my research questions and are in keeping with my worldview as a researcher. This research is exploratory — looking at a group that has had little attention in the past — and is highly contextual, focusing on the realm of surgical training.

I bring to this research a feminist, post-positivist worldview. I see reality as being subjectively created by each individual; rich, complex, multiple, and interconnected. Our interactions with others and with the world are unavoidably molded by our perceptions, values, understandings, histories, culture, prior experiences, and context. Yet we exist within a web of connection and inter-relatedness.

In the generation of knowledge, this research falls generally within the ethnographic culture of inquiry and, more specifically, within heuristic research influenced by feminist critical ethnography. I am interested in the experiences of women living at the intersection of gender, race, and male privilege. Surgery has long been the quintessential male domain, the stronghold of male privilege within the profession of medicine. What has been the experience of these women in residency? How do they make sense of the culture of surgery? How do they make sense of their lives within this context? These understandings will best be achieved through ethnographic case studies.

Qualitative research and ethnography have been discussed in a number of texts.[1] Atkinson and Hammersley (in Denzin & Lincoln) characterized ethnography as follows:

> In practical terms, ethnography usually refers to forms of social research having a substantial number of the following features:
>
> - a strong emphasis on exploring the nature of particular social phenomena, rather than setting out to test hypotheses about them
>
> - a tendency to work primarily with "unstructured" data, that is, data that have not been coded at the point of data collection in terms of a closed set of analytic categories
>
> - investigation of a small number of cases, perhaps just one case, in detail
>
> - analysis of data that involves explicit interpretation of the meanings and functions of human actions, the product of which mainly takes the form of verbal descriptions and explanations, with quantification and statistical analysis playing a subordinate role at most.[2]

The influence of race on — and a critical analysis of race and ethnicity in — research methods is provided by Facio and Stanfield.[3] Critical ethnography as delineated by Thomas takes conventional ethnography into the realm of action and social change. This perspective unapologetically takes the stance that research should be emancipatory and proceeds from this explicit value.

Critical ethnography begins from the premise that knowledge is a resource as powerful as any tangible tool. As a tool, new ways of thinking become implements by which we can *act upon* our world instead of passively being *acted upon*. We can affect our own personal development and that of our surroundings only when we have a reasonably clear view of the nature of our culture and what possibilities for action are open to us. Critical ethnography attempts to provide clearer images of the larger picture of which we are a part. Once the picture takes on sharper detail, opportunities for revising it take shape.[4]

Feminist theory is a subset of critical ethnography that operates from a core of feminist values, awarenesses, and critical analyses. It includes a commitment to avoiding sexism in research.[5] The feminist perspective in this research is influenced by Black feminist thought and feminist values as discussed by Black and White feminists. The identification of *Black* feminist thought is important, since little consideration was given to race, or other dimensions of structural oppression, in the initial theoretical analyses of White feminists. As bell hooks stated:

Like Friedan before them, White women who dominate feminist discourse today rarely question whether or not their perspective on women's reality is true to the lived experiences of women as a collective group. Nor are they aware of the extent to which their perspectives reflect race and class biases, although there has been a greater awareness of biases in recent years. Racism abounds in the writings of White feminists, reinforcing White supremacy and negating the possibility that women will bond politically across ethnic and racial boundaries. Past feminist refusal to draw attention to and attack racial hierarchies suppressed the link between race and class.[6]

In *Teaching to Transgress,* hooks discussed the shift in feminist theory:

> The efforts of Black women and Women of Color to challenge and deconstruct the category "woman" — the insistence on recognition that gender is not the sole factor determining constructions of femaleness — was a critical intervention, one which led to a profound revolution in feminist thought and truly interrogated and disrupted the hegemonic feminist theory produced primarily by academic women, most of whom were White.[7]

Collins defined Black feminist thought and some underlying assumptions:

> Black feminist thought consists of ideas produced by Black women that clarify a standpoint of and for Black women.... First, the definition suggests that it is impossible to separate the structure and thematic content of thought from the historical and material conditions shaping the lives of its producers. Therefore, while Black feminist thought may be recorded by others, it is produced by Black women. Second, the definition assumes that Black women possess a unique standpoint on, or perspective of, their experiences and that there will be certain commonalities of perception shared by Black women as a group. Third, while living life as Black women may produce certain commonalities of outlook, the diversity of class, age, region, and sexual orientation shaping individual

> Black women's lives has resulted in different expres-
> sions of these common themes…. Finally, the defi-
> nition assumes that, while a Black woman's stand-
> point exists, its contours may not be clear to Black
> women themselves. Therefore, one role for Black
> female intellectuals is to produce facts and theories
> about the Black female experience that will clarify a
> Black woman's standpoint for Black women.[8]

She went on to define three key themes in Black feminist thought. First is the meaning of self-definition and self-valuation. "Self-definition involves challenging the political knowledge-validation process that has resulted in externally-defined stereotypical images of Afro-American womanhood. In contrast, self-valuation stresses the content of Black women's self-definitions — namely, replacing externally-derived images with authentic Black female images."

Collins' second key theme is that of attention to the interlocking nature of oppression — race, gender, and class. She wrote:

> As Barbara Smith points out [in *Home Girls*, 1983,
> New York: Kitchen Table, Women of Color Press],
> "…the concept of the simultaneity of oppression is
> still the crux of a Black feminist understanding of
> political reality and…is one of the most significant
> ideological contributions of Black feminist thought."
> This should come as no surprise since Black women
> should be among the first to realize that minimizing
> one form of oppression, while essential, may still leave
> them oppressed in other equally dehumanizing ways.[8]

This perspective shifts the focus away from the temptation to develop a hierarchy of oppressions to a more holistic, systemic understanding.

In the third key theme, Collins emphasized the importance of redefining Black women's culture. This theme understands culture to be a mobile, changing frame of reference strongly influenced by context.

> While common themes may link Black women's lives, these themes will be experienced differently by Black women of different classes, ages, regions, and sexual preferences as well as by Black women in different historical settings. Thus, there is no monolithic Black women's culture — rather, there are socially-constructed Black women's cultures that collectively form Black women's culture.[8]

Hooks wrote about the transformative power of feminist theory:

> Reflecting on my own work in feminist theory, I find writing — theoretical talk — to be most meaningful when it invites readers to engage in critical reflection and to engage in the practice of feminism. To me, this theory emerges from the concrete, from my efforts to make sense of everyday life experiences, from my efforts to intervene critically in my life and the lives of others. This to me is what makes feminist transformation possible. Personal testimony, personal experience, is such fertile ground for the production of liberatory feminist theory because it usually forms the base of our theory making.[7]

It is this possibility of liberatory feminist theory that drives this research for me.

Feminist values bring to research methodologies a critical focus on the potential inherent power differentials in research and the potential for research to exploit the subjects. Riger quoted Mary Gergen's central tenets of a feminist method:

- recognizing the interdependence of experimenter and subject;

- avoiding the decontextualizing of the subject or experimenter from their social and historical surroundings;

- recognizing and revealing the natures of one's values within the research context;

- accepting that facts do not exist independently of their producers' linguistic codes;

- demystifying the role of the scientist and establishing an egalitarian relationship between science makers and science consumers.[9]

A similar set of strategies or methods for "practical implementation of a feminist perspective in social science research" is offered by Jayaratine and Stewart (in Fonow and Cook). Olesen provided a more conceptual overview of feminist perspectives in research in her discussion of the diverse models, methods, approaches, and epistemologies of feminist research.[10]

While the general culture of my research is ethnographic, and the philosophical influences are feminist research, the specific methodology utilized is heuristic research as described by Moustakas. This is uniquely suited to this research because of the emphasis on the autobiographical and the personal (self-search, self-dialogue and self-discovery) in interaction with the research data to create new knowledge.

Heuristic research has several underlying concepts/processes. Forming the infrastructure in heuristic research is the importance of tacit knowing. Tacit knowing is the complement of explicit knowing and "allows one to sense the unity or wholeness of something from an understanding of the individual qualities or parts." Intuition acts as a bridge between the explicit and the tacit.

> In intuition, from the subsidiary or observable factors one utilizes an internal capacity to make inferences and arrive at a knowledge of underlying structures or dynamics. Intuition makes immediate knowledge possible without the intervening steps of logic and reasoning. While the tacit is pure mystery in its focal nature — ineffable and unspecifiable — in the intuitive process one draws on clues; one senses a pattern or underlying condition that enables one to imagine and then characterize the reality, state of mind, or condition. In intuition we perceive something, observe it, and look and look again from clue to clue until we surmise the truth.[11]

Indwelling and focusing are the heuristic processes of creating a receptive inward space and "...turning inward to seek a deeper, more extended comprehension of the nature or meaning of a quality or theme of human experience.... The indwelling process is conscious and deliberate, yet it is not lineal or logical. It follows clues wherever they appear; one dwells inside them and expands their meanings and associations until a fundamental insight is achieved." Focusing then moves one deeper into the experience:

> The focusing process enables the researcher to identify qualities of an experience that have remained out of conscious reach primarily because the individual has not paused long enough to examine his or her

experience of the phenomenon. Through the focusing process, the researcher is able to determine the core themes that constitute an experience, identify and assess connecting feelings and thoughts, and achieve cognitive knowledge that includes refinements of meaning and perception that register as internal shifts and alterations of behavior.[11]

These processes enable the researcher to move toward "the ultimate creative synthesis that portrays the essential qualities and meanings of an experience."

Moustakas identified six phases of heuristic research:

- Initial engagement — discovery of an intense interest with important social meanings and personal, compelling implications resulting in the formulation of a research question.

- Immersion — living within the question and coming to be on intimate terms with it. This is facilitated through the use of spontaneous self-dialogue and self-searching, pursuing intuitive clues or hunches, and drawing from the mystery and sources of energy and knowledge within the tacit dimension.

- Incubation — a retreat from the intense, concentrated focus on the question which enables the inner tacit dimension to reach its full possibilities in continuing to clarify and extend understanding on levels outside the immediate awareness.

- Illumination — a breakthrough into conscious awareness of qualities and a clustering of qualities into themes inherent in the question; the opening of a door to a new awareness, a modification of an old understanding, a synthesis of fragmented knowledge, or a new discovery of something that has been present for some time yet beyond immediate awareness.

- Explication — full examination of what has been awakened in consciousness in order to understand its various layers of meaning, utilizing focusing, indwelling, self-searching, and self-disclosure.

- Creative synthesis — utilization of tacit and intuitive powers to permit an inward life on the question to grow and realize a comprehensive expression of the essences of the phenomenon under investigation.[11]

In the process of heuristic research the question of validity is one of meaning. "Does the ultimate depiction of the experience derived from one's own rigorous, exhaustive self-searching and from the explications of others present comprehensively, vividly, and accurately the meanings and essences of the experience?" The researcher repeatedly checks the depictions of the experience against the data. This "appraisal of significance" and "checking and judging...enable the researcher to achieve repeated verification that the explication of the phenomenon and the creative synthesis of essences and meanings actually portray the phenomenon investigated." This is enhanced by sharing the meanings and essences of the phenomenon with the participants for their assessment of its completeness in capturing their experiences.

It is clear to me that both heuristic research and feminist theorizing are inherently concerned with the generation of knowledge and with personal transformation. Successful work results in both the researcher and the participants experiencing personal transformation. My research contributes to professional practice by voicing the impact of training on these women surgeons, by bringing to light an experience previously undocumented, and providing a perspective previously unexplored. This will be of value to women surgeons — Black and White; other women physicians; those interested in physicians' training — both as educators and as potential patients; students of women in nontraditional professions; and women of color in a variety of personal and professional roles, to name a few.

Participant Identification and Selection

In planning participant identification and selection I chose to restrict the study group to Black female general surgeons. The addition of other surgical subspecialties — cardiothoracic, plastic surgery, orthopedics, etc. — would have increased the variability in the group related to different types of residency experiences and increased the amount of potentially confounding data related to the additional training years. I estimated that there would be about twenty-five Black women general surgeons practicing in the United States. I anticipated that the limited number of individuals in this group would make participant selection relatively straightforward. Since the focus of the research is on the residency experience, I wanted the participants to meet the following five criteria:

- Black women who have completed a certified general surgery residency program;

- practicing general surgeons;

- between five and fifteen years out of residency training;

- American Board of Surgery–qualified or eligible;

- representing geographic variety in place of practice.

The time from training was selected to identify participants with some temporal distance from their residency experience who were similar with respect to age and when they completed residency training. I wanted to screen out the earliest pioneers and the most recent graduates to identify potential participants whose experiences occurred within a defined period and context. Board certification or eligibility helped identify women who trained in accredited programs. Geographic variability helped to avoid bias on the basis of regional idiosyncrasies in residency programs.

Participants for this research were identified a) by letters sent to five professional organizations and a known researcher in this area; b) by my personal knowledge; and c) by word of mouth. An introductory letter and a brief survey (Appendices A, B), soliciting demographic data and willingness to participate in a face-to-face interview, were sent to all identified Black female general surgeons. The survey was used to identify a potential participant subgroup of Black female general surgeons who met the research criteria, were willing to be interviewed, and were accessible to me.

Data Collection Procedures

One hundred ten surveys and informed consent forms (Appendix C) were mailed with stamped, pre-addressed envelopes enclosed for responses. Survey information was tabulated and analyzed. Aggregate information is discussed earlier.

Six "dialogue"[11] interviews (Appendix D) were performed with the women identified as willing to be participants. Informed consent was obtained from the participants (Appendix E), and all interview material was kept anonymous. Participants were able to decline participation in interviews via the survey instrument and were informed, in the consent form and at the time of the interview, that they could terminate participation at any time. Consent forms also had a box where participants could indicate their interest in receiving a copy of the completed dissertation. Interviews lasted approximately an hour and a half and were performed at sites convenient to me and to the interviewees. The interview transcript and my individual depiction were sent to each participant for her review and comment. The interview participants will be invited to participate, with other interested Black women surgeons, in a discussion of the study findings that will be scheduled in concert with a national surgical meeting.

Potential benefits to the participants included a) an opportunity to reflect on personal experiences; b) an opportunity to be seen and heard in a possibly new way; c) "debriefing" of a significant developmental life experience; and d) an opportunity to collaborate in the creation of new knowledge. Potential risks to the participants might have included the remembering of traumatic or stressful situations and experiences. It was unlikely that significant psychological or emotional distress would result from this; in fact, this type of experience has been shown to be helpful in relieving post-traumatic stress.[12] If a participant had experienced distress during the interview process, my training as a physician, in Gestalt therapy, and with National Training Laboratories would have qualified me to provide assistance. No participant reported distress during the process.

The process of the interview relied on the development of a relationship between me (the interviewer) and the woman participant. As discussed by Fontana and Frey (in Denzin & Lincoln):

> As Oakley points out, in interviewing there is "no intimacy without reciprocity." Thus the emphasis is shifting to allow the development of a closer relation

between interviewer and respondent, attempting to minimize status differences and doing away with the traditional hierarchical situation in interviewing. Interviewers can show their human side and answer questions and express feelings. Methodologically, this new approach provides a greater spectrum of responses and a greater insight into respondents — or participants, to avoid the hierarchical pitfall — because it encourages them to control the sequencing and the language of the interview and also allows them the freedom of open-ended responses.[2]

Moustakas further characterized the heuristic interview as a dialogue that involves cooperative sharing.

In heuristic interviewing, the data generated is dependent upon accurate, empathic listening; being open to oneself and to the co-researcher; being flexible and free to vary procedures to respond to what is required in the flow of dialogue; and being skillful in creating a climate that encourages the co-researcher to respond comfortably, accurately, comprehensively, and honestly in elucidating the phenomenon.[11]

Clearly, my dual status as a Black female surgeon and as a social science researcher was an advantage to me in engaging in these dialogues. Similarity of history gave me and the participants a common ground on which to build our intimacy. Years of clinical practice have also given me experience in developing relationships in a limited time frame; NTL Laboratories and Gestalt training have given me insight into interpersonal dynamics. The dialogic nature of the interviews and the use of feminist methodologies that provided opportunities for the participants to review the transcripts and data have assisted me in avoiding bias.

Data Analysis Procedures

Interviews were tape recorded and transcribed as they were completed. Field notes were completed immediately following each interview to capture my subjective impressions of the participant, the interview process, and the environment. I also kept a reflective journal in which I recorded my process self-dialogues, self-searching, and emotional responses to this work.

Data analysis was ongoing, using the process developed by Moustakas.[11] When completed, a transcript of the interview and my depiction was sent to each participant for review, verification, and collaboration, making the work a collective enterprise. Only two participants responded with comments. The interview voices, interpretations, and comments have been woven into a personal, group, and theoretical understanding.

Several steps were taken to ensure the accuracy or validity of this study. Meticulous care was taken in listening, recording, transcribing, noting, and analyzing the data. Involvement of the participants in reading the materials was supplemented by the involvement of colleagues in looking for factual or conceptual errors. Participants have been given the opportunity to obtain copies of the final results and/or the completed dissertation. My personal reflections as a Black woman general surgeon and as a researcher provide a mechanism for critical analysis.

Summary

In summary, I used the qualitative methods of heuristic and feminist research to investigate the impact of the residency experience on a sample of Black women general surgeons. I listened to their stories of their residency experiences and how they have subsequently made meaning of them, and from this I developed an enhanced understanding of the impact of these formative years. My goal was the development of therapeutic liberatory theory that can be used to assist surgical residents, other physicians in training, and training program personnel. As bell hooks wrote:

> I came to theory because I was hurting — the pain within me was so intense that I could not go on living. I came to theory desperate, wanting to comprehend — to grasp what was happening around and within me. Most importantly, I wanted to make the hurt go away. I saw in theory then a location for healing.

> I found a place of sanctuary in "theorizing," in making sense out of what was happening. I found a place where I could imagine possible futures, a place where life could be lived differently. This "lived" experience of critical thinking, of reflection and analysis, became a place where I worked at explaining the hurt and making it go away.

> Catharine MacKinnon reminds us that "we know things with our lives and we live that knowledge, beyond what any theory has yet theorized (sic). Making this theory is the challenge before us. For in its production lies the hope of our liberation, in its production lies the possibility of naming all our pain

— of making all our hurt go away. If we create feminist theory, feminist movements that address this pain, we will have no difficulty building a mass-based feminist resistance struggle. There will be no gap between feminist theory and feminist practice.[7]

Chapter 7

Conclusions

Personal Meaning

This research clearly has both personal and professional meaning for me. I was fully engaged in all aspects of the experience. I felt the same kind of anticipation about making initial contact with potential participants via the survey as I would sending invitations to a party. When I compiled and tabulated the survey data I felt that I was discovering a community of women unlike any other I had known. I was excited to learn something of their lives: their ages, their parents' occupations, their educational experiences, and the factors that influenced their choice of surgery. These elements thrilled me with the similarities to and differences from my own history.

In the role of interviewer I was challenged by the tension between the familiar and the unfamiliar. The familiar contact with a professional colleague, the unfamiliar experience of that colleague being the same race and gender as myself, the newness of talking about personal residency experiences, and the unfamiliar experience of myself as a doctoral researcher.

The facets of experience that I describe in this work are still alive for me today. As the material from the interviews was coming to life I became aware of my own use of distancing in my current life. During the writing I was dealing concurrently with my mother having a stroke, major family disturbances, a chaotic work environment, and the usual stresses of breast surgery practice. I was simultaneously writing about distancing and becoming fully aware of how intensely I was practicing it. There are days when I am so immersed in my work that I can find little time for family or community. Then I start to surface again and attempt to find more balance.

As I have matured in my practice of surgery, I find that the experience of transcendence still occurs in the operating room, but I also find it in the exam room when I am developing a relationship with a patient and helping her to move through the life-changing experience of breast cancer.

I have learned an immense amount in doing this research. It has provided me with tremendous insights into my own residency experience and helped me to find the words and concepts to make meaning of it. It has also provided me with a new community of Black women general surgeons in place of my previously isolated environment.

Implications

This research describes several previously undocumented phenomena that have relevance to surgical and medical educators; patients seeking more humanistic care; those seeking to understand the development of or lack of empathy in physicians; surgeons themselves; students of Black women's experiences; and those interested in the experiencing of racism and sexism. It opens a door on the experiences of a virtually unexamined group of Black women.

This work has only opened the door into Black female surgeons' experiences a small crack. It would be invaluable to follow their experiences as they move into their careers and assess the impact of race and gender on their work lives. It would be useful to understand how their outlooks and actions are impacted by their developing awareness of inequities during their periods of surfacing. It would be fascinating to see if the perception that gender has more significance than race in surgery holds, as more White women become surgeons and as Black women enter practice settings.

Future research could build on this work by exploring the experiences of other subgroups of surgeons (White women, Black men, Hispanic women, etc.) to better understand their residencies and to see if there are common experiences. I would like to see more research into the phenomenon of distancing, both to better understand its utility as a coping mechanism and to understand the impact it has on surgeons' lives in general. It would be useful to explore the tension, if any, between distancing and the development of compassion and empathy.

This work can also be used to inform surgical residency programs. Some of the interviewees offered their vision of ideal residency programs, and hoped that their voices could play a role in the humanization of surgical residencies. While they appreciated the value of an intense surgical education, they longed for more supports. Suggestions included onsite child care, mentoring, having other Black female surgeons as role models, and utilizing methodologies such as critical incident debriefing to assist residents in acknowledging and processing the emotional impact of traumatic residency experiences.

Critical incident debriefing is a technique that has been demonstrated to reduce the occurrence of post-traumatic stress syndromes. It simply provides individuals and groups with the opportunity to talk over the stressful event. That healing can result from being heard has been well documented.[1] The Black Women's Health Project, a national organization, uses a very successful technique of self-help groups. They have shown that being heard is a powerful healing experience. "Having voice," having one's reality witnessed by others, can open the way for dissolution of pain, enhancement of understanding, and integration of meaning. The addition of this simple intervention could have a major impact on improving the lives of residents.

Another valuable offshoot of this study would be to look at the experiences of women — Black, White, Asian, Latina — in other male-dominated professions to see how their experiences compare with those of Black women surgeons. The finding that gender appeared to be more significant than race for many of these participants indicates the need for more research into the impact of gender bias on professional women of all races.

These stories are a testament to the determination, courage, and resilience of the participants, each of whom can serve as a role model for others coming behind her. These Black women surgeons wanted to tell their stories so that Black women surgery residents could learn from them and have the strength and vision to move forward. Hooks reminds us that "We are sustained by one another's testimony when we find ourselves faltering or falling into despair."[2]

Each of these stories is an element in the collective self-recovery process of Black women surgeons. In presenting them and the rest of my research to surgical communities and groups of Black women surgeons and physicians, I hope to facilitate more opportunities for us to develop community — to tell our stories, and to witness the stories of others. As hooks wrote:

> Again and again, when I talk with Black women who are engaged in a recovery and liberation process...I hear from all of us a concern about building a greater sense of community. It was maybe four years ago that I sat with Ntozake Shange and raised this question in relation to Black women: "Where is the healing place?" Now, I am more confident that community is the healing place. As Black women come together with one another, with all the other folks in the world who are seeking recovery and liberation, we find the will to be well affirmed, we find ways to get what we need to ease the pain, to make the hurt go away. Some of us are more involved in structured recovery programs, in intense ongoing therapy, others of us do a lot of "home psychoanalysis" (my term for the therapy that friends, comrades and loved ones can do together daily). We are all discovering that the experience of community is crucial to wellness.[2]

Endnotes

Chapter 1. Opening the Door to Understanding

1. Reid, P., & Kelly, E. "Research on Women of Color: From Ignorance to Awareness," *Psychology of Women Quarterly* 18 (1994): 477-486.

Chapter 2. What's been studied about women and minorities in medicine

1. Freidson, E., & Lorber, J. *Medical Men and their Work* (Chicago: Aldine Atherton, 1972); Becker, H., Geer, B., Hughes, E., & Strauss, A. *Boys in White: Student Culture in Medical School* (Chicago: The University of Chicago Press, 1961); Bynam, J. "Medical School Socialization and the New Physician: Role, Status, Adjustments, Personal Problems, and Social Identity," *Psychological Reprints* 57 (1985): 182; Conrad, P. "Learning to Doctor: Reflections on Recent Accounts of the Medical School Years," *Journal of Health and Social Behavior* 29 (1988): 323-332; Coombs, R. *Mastering Medicine: Professional Socialization in Medical School* (New York: The Free Press, 1978), p.190; Glasser, R. *Ward 402* (New York: George Braziller, 1973); Mumford, E. *Interns: From Students to Physicians* (Cambridge, MA: Harvard University Press, 1970); Shuval, J. "From 'Boy' to 'Colleague': Processes of Role Transformation in Professional Socialization," *Social Science & Medicine* 9 (1975): 413-420.

2. Bickel, J. "Women in Medical Education: A Status Report," *New England Journal of Medicine* 319 (1988): 1579-1584; Braslow, J., & Heins, M. "Women in Medical Education: A Decade of Change," *New England Journal of Medicine* 304 (1981): 1129-1135; Diamond, E. "Women in Medicine: Two Points of View I. The Future of Women Physicians," *JAMA,*

249 (1983): 207-208; Eisenberg, C. "Women as Physicians," *J. Medical Education, 58* (1983): 534-541; Heins, M. "Women in Medicine: Two Points of View II. Medicine and Motherhood," *JAMA, 249* (1983): 209-210; Kris, K. "Developmental Strains of Female Medical Students," *JAMA, 40* (1983): 145-148; Lorber, J. *Women Physicians: Careers, Status, and Power* (New York: Tavistock Publications, 1984); Mandelbaum-Schmid, J. "Women and Medicine: Are Some Doctors Less Equal than Others?" *MD* (1992, February): 73-80; Mandelbaum-Schmid, J. "Women and Medicine: Are Women Physicians Changing the Practice of Medicine?" *MD* (1992, March): 69-74; Mandelbaum-Schmid, J. "Women and Medicine: An Unequal Past, a Common Future," *MD* (1992, May): 87-98; Martin, S., Parker, R., & Arnold, R. "Careers of Women Physicians: Choices and Constraints," in Women and Medicine (Special Issue), *Western Journal of Medicine 149* (1988): 758-760; Notman, M., & Nadelson, C. "Medicine: A Career Conflict for Women," *American J. Psychiatry 130* (1973): 1123-1127; Ortiz, F. "Women in Medicine: The Process of Professional Incorporation," *JAMWA, 30* (1975): 18-30; Anonymous. "The Goal," *JAMA, 250* (1983): 407; Anonymous. "Does Anybody Hear?" *JAMWA, 49* (1994): 92-93; Ducker, D. "Research on Women Physicians with Multiple Roles: A Feminist Perspective," *JAMWA, 49* (1994): 78-84; Osborne, D. "My Wife, the Doctor: Have Women Humanized Medicine?" *This World* (1983, April 3): 8-10; Wear, D., ed. *Women in Medical Education: An Anthology of Experience* (Albany, NY: State University of New York Press, 1996).

3. Baldwin, D., Daugherty, S., & Rowley, B. "Racial and Ethnic Discrimination During Residency: Results of a National Survey," *Acad Med 69* (1994): 519-21; Cregler, L., Clark, L., & Jackson, E. "Careers in Academic Medicine and Clinical Practice for Minorities: Opportunities and Barriers," *J Assoc Acad Minor Phys 5* (1994): 68-73; Pamies, R., Lawrence, L., Helm E., & Strayhorn G. "The Effects of Certain Student and Institutional Characteristics on Minority Medical Student Specialty Choice," *J. Natl Med Assoc 86* (1994): 136-40;

Campos-Outcalt, D., Rutala, P., Witzke, D., & Fulginiti, J. "Performances of Underrepresented-Minority Students at the University of Arizona College of Medicine, 1987–1991," *Acad Med* 69 (1994): 577-82; Webb, C., Herbert, J., & Waugh, F. "Predictors of Black Students' Board Performances: MCAT Scores Are Not the Whole Story [letter]," *Acad Med* 68 (1993): 204-205; Webb, C., Waugh, F., & Herbert, J. "Relationship Between Locus of Control and Performance on the National Board of Medical Examiners, Part I, Among Black Medical Students," *Psychol Rep* 72 (1993): 1171-1177; Martin, M. "Applicant Pool for Emergency Medicine Residency Programs: Information on Minority and Female Applicants," *Ann Emerg Med* 27 (1996): 331-338; Organ, C. "Good News in the Greenvilles of America [editorial]," *Arch Surg* 130 (1995): 1033-1034; Epps, R.P. "The Black Woman Physician," *J. Natl Med Assoc* 78 (1985): 375-381; Goodwin, N. "The Black Woman Physician," *NY State J of Medicine* (1985, April): 145-147; Organ, C., & Kosiba, M. *A Century of Black Surgeons: The U.S. Experience* (Norman, OK: Transcript Press, 1987), 588, 590, 609.

4. Yogev, S., & Harris, S. "Women Physicians During Residency Years: Workload, Work Satisfaction and Self-Concept," *Soc. Sci. Med* 17 (1983): 837.

5. U.S. Department of Health and Human Services, Public Health Service, Council on Graduate Medical Education. *Fifth Report: Women & Medicine* (HRSA-P-DM-95-1). (Washington, DC: U.S. Government Printing Office 1995), 31, 33-35, 41.

6. Notman, M., & Nadelson, C. "Medicine: A Career Conflict for Women," *Amer J. Psychiatry* 130 (1973): 1123-1127.

7. Baldwin, D., Daugherty, S., & Rowley, B. "Racial and Ethnic Discrimination During Residency: Results of a National Survey," *Acad Med* 69 (1994): 519-521.

8. Goodwin, N. "The Black Woman Physician," *NY State J of Medicine* (1985, April): 145-147.

9. Epps, R. "The Black Woman Physician," *J. Natl Med Assoc 78* (1985): 375-381.

10. Haug, J. "A Review of Women in Surgery," *Bulletin of the American College of Surgery* 60 (1975): 21-23; Sheldon, G. "Recruitment and Selection of the Best and Brightest," *Ann Thoracic Surgery* 55(5) (1993, May): 1340-1344; U.S. Department of Health and Human Services, Public Health Service, Council on Graduate Medical Education. *Fifth Report: Women & Medicine* (HRSA-P-DM-95-1). (Washington, DC: U.S. Government Printing Office 1995), 31, 33-35, 41; Martin, S., Parker, R. & Arnold, R. "Careers of Women Physicians: Choices and Constraints," in Women and Medicine (Special Issue), *Western J. Medicine* 149 (1988): 758-760.

11. Moore, F., & Priebe, C. "Board-Certified Physicians in the United States, 1971–1986," *New England Journal of Medicine* 324 (1991): 536-543.

12. McNamara, M. "Women Surgeons: How Much of an Impact?" *Curr Surg* 42 (1985): 94-100.

13. Cohen, M., Woodward, C., & Ferrier, B. "Factors Influencing Career Development: Do Men and Women Differ?" *JAMWA, 43* (1988): 142-154.

14. Walters, B. "Why Don't More Women Choose Surgery as a Career?" *Acad Med* 68 (1993): 350-351.

15. Ortiz, R. "Women in Medicine: The Process of Professional Incorporation," *JAMWA, 30* (1975): 18-30.

16. Gabram, S.G., Allen, L.W., & Deckers, P.J. "Surgical Residents in the 1990s: Issues and Concerns for Men and Women," *Arch Surg* 130(1) (1995, Jan.): 24-28.

17. Maran, A., Cudworth, J., Doig, C., & Wilson, J. "Women in Surgery in Scotland: A Working Party of the Royal College of Surgeons of Edinburgh." *J R Coll Surg Edinb* 38(5) (1993, Oct.): 279-284; Neumayer, L., Konishi, G., L'Archeveque, D., Choi, R., Ferrario, T., McGrath, J., Nakawatase, T., Freischlag, J., & Levison, W. "Female Surgeons in the 1990s: Academic

Role Models," *Archives of Surgery* 128 (1993): 669-672; Jonasson, O. "Women as Leaders in Organized Surgery and Surgical Education: Has the Time Come?" *Archives of Surgery* 128 (1993): 618-621; Bickel, J. "Women in Medical Education: A Status Report," *New England J Medicine* 319 (1988): 1579-1584.

18. Eskenazi, L., & Weston, J. "The Pregnant Plastic Surgical Resident: Results of a Survey of Women Plastic Surgeons and Plastic Surgery Residency Directors," *Plast Reconstr Surg* 95 (1995): 330-355; Guth, C. "Pregnancy and Residency [letter: comment]," *Plast Reconstr Surg* 93 (1994): 889; MacKinnon, S., & Mizgala, C. "Pregnancy and Plastic Surgery Residency [editorial]," *Plast Reconstr Surg* 94 (1994): 186-192; Wray, R. "Pregnancy and Plastic Surgery Residency [editorial]," *Plast Reconstr Surg* 91 (1993): 344-345; Young-Shumate, L., Kramer, T., & Beresin, E. "Pregnancy During Graduate Medical Training," *Acad Med* 86 (1993): 792-799; Ramos, S. & Feiner, C. "Women Surgeons: A National Survey," *JAMWA*, 44 (1989): 21-25.

19. Organ, C. & Kosiba, M. *A Century of Black Surgeons: The U.S. Experience* (Norman, OK: Transcript Press, 1987), 609, 590.

Chapter 3.   What surgical residencies are like

1. Kinder, B. "Women and Men as Surgeons: Are the Problems Really Different?" *Current Surgery* 42 (1985): 100-104.

2. Coombs, R. *Mastering Medicine: Professional Socialization in Medical School* (New York: The Free Press, 1978), p. 190.

3. Pasterna, J. "Women in Surgery: An Ancient Tradition," *Archives of Surgery* 128 (1993): 622-626.

4. Sandrick, K. "The Residency Experience: The Woman's Perspective," *American College of Surgeons Bulletin* 77 (1992): 10-17.

5. Dreyfuss, J.H. "Although Number of Women Surgeons Grows, Women Still Face Many Challenges in Surgery," *General Surgery & Laparoscopy News* (1995, Sept): 1, 18-19; "How to Swim with Sharks," *Association of Women Surgeons Newsletter* 7 (1995): 9.

Chapter 5.   Understanding the residency experience

1. Addison, R. "Surviving the Residency: A Grounded Interpretive Investigation of Physician Socialization," unpublished doctoral dissertation, University of California, Berkeley (Order No. DA84-26889), *Dissertation Abstracts International* 45 (1984): 3111; Shem, S. *The House of God* (New York: Marek, 1978); Mizrahi, T. *Getting Rid of Patients: Contradictions in the Socialization of Physicians* (New Brunswick, NJ: Rutgers University Press, 1986), 84, 195; Cherniss, C. *Beyond Burnout* (New York: Routledge, 1995).

2. Mizrahi, T. *Getting Rid of Patients: Contradictions in the Socialization of Physicians* (New Brunswick, NJ: Rutgers University Press, 1986), 84, 195.

3. Butcher, J. *Abnormal Psychology* (Belmont, CA: Brooks/Cole Publishing Co., 1971).

4. Meichenbaum, D., Price, R., Phares, E.J., McCormick, N., & Hyde, J. *Exploring Choices — The Psychology of Adjustment* (Boston, MA: Scott, Foresman and Co., 1989), 169.

5. Bromberg, P. "Shadow and Substance: A Relational Perspective on Clinical Process," *Psychoanalytic Psychology* 10 (1993): 147-168; Bromberg, P. "Speak! That I May See You: Some Reflections on Dissociation, Reality and Psychoanalytic Listening," *Psychoanalytic Dialogues* 4 (1994): 517-547; Bromberg, P. "Standing in the Spaces: The Multiplicity of Self and the Psychoanalytic Relationship," *Contemporary Psychoanalysis* 32 (1996): 509-535.

6. Lazarus, R., & Lazarus, B. *Passion and Reason: Making Sense of Our Emotions* (New York: Oxford University Press, 1994), 164.

7. Green, G., Wilson, J., & Lindy, J. "Conceptualizing Post-Traumatic Stress Disorder: A Psychosocial Framework," in C.R. Figley (Ed.), *Trauma and Its Wake* (New York: Brunner/Mazel, 1985), 53-69; Parson, E. "Ethnicity and Traumatic Stress: The Intersecting Point in Psychotherapy," in C.R. Figley (Ed.), *Trauma and Its Wake* (New York: Brunner/Mazel, 1985), 314-337; Scrignar, C. *Post-Traumatic Stress Disorder*, Second Edition (New Orleans, LA: Bruno Press, 1988); Wilson, J., Smith, W.K., & Johnson, S. "A Comparative Analysis of PTSD Among Various Survivor Groups," in C.R. Figley (Ed.), *Trauma and Its Wake* (New York: Brunner/Mazel, 1985), 142-172.

8. Janoff-Bulman, R. *Shattered Assumptions: Towards a New Psychology of Trauma* (New York: The Free Press, 1992), 95, 97-100.

9. Comas-Dias, L., & Greene, B. (Eds.). *Women of Color: Integrating Ethnic and Gender Identities in Psychotherapy* (New York: The Guilford Press, 1994); Cross, E., Katz, J., Miller, F., & Seashore, E. (Eds.). *The Promise of Diversity* (New York: Irwin Publishing, 1994); Pinderhughes, E. *Understanding Race, Ethnicity, and Power* (New York: The Free Press, 1989); Sue, D.W., & Sue, D. *Counseling the Culturally Different* (New York: John Wiley & Sons, 1990); McGoldrick, M., Garcia-Preto, N., Moore Hines, P., & Lee, E. "Ethnicity and Women," in M. McGoldrick, C. Anderson & Walsh, F. (Eds.), *Women in Families* (New York: W.W. Norton & Co., 1989), 169-199; Essed, P. *Understanding Everyday Racism: An Interdisciplinary Theory* (Newbury Park, CA: Sage Publications, 1991), 35-36; Kanter, R. *Men and Women of the Corporation* (New York: Basic Books, 1977); hooks, b. *Sisters of the Yam: Black Women and Self-Recovery* (Boston, MA: South End Press, 1993), 133.

10. McGoldrick, M., Garcia-Preto, N., Moore Hines, P., & Lee, E. "Ethnicity and Women," in M. McGoldrick, C. Anderson & Walsh, F. (Eds.), *Women in Families* (New York: W.W. Norton & Co., 1989), 169-199.

11. Essed, P. *Understanding Everyday Racism: An Interdisciplinary Theory* (Newbury Park, CA: Sage Publications, 1991), 35-36.

12. hooks, b. *Sisters of the Yam: Black Women and Self-Recovery* (Boston, MA: South End Press, 1993), 133.

13. Young-Eisendrath, P. *The Resilient Spirit: Transforming Suffering into Insight and Renewal* (New York: Addison-Wesley Publishing Co., Inc., 1996), 7, 48.

14. O'Connell, A., & O'Connell, V. *Choice and Change: The Psychology of Holistic Growth, Adjustment, and Creativity* (Englewood Cliffs, NJ: Prentice Hall, 1992), 422.

15. Csikszentmihalyi, M. *Flow: The Psychology of Optimal Experience* (New York: HarperPerennial, 1990), 49.

16. Epps, R.P. "The Black Woman Physician," *J Natl Med Assoc* 78 (1985): 375-381.

17. McNamara, M. "Women Surgeons: How Much of an Impact?" *Curr Surg* 42 (1985): 94-100.

18. Ortiz, F. "Women in Medicine: The Process of Professional Incorporation," *JAMWA, 30* (1975): 18-30.

19. Kinder, B. "Women and Men as Surgeons: Are the Problems Really Different?" *Curr Surg* 42 (1985): 100-104.

20. Sterling, R. "Female Surgeons: The Dawn of a New Era," in C.H. Organ & M. Kosiba (Eds.), *A Century of Black Surgeons: The U.S. Experience* (Norman, OK: Transcript Press, 1987), 581-610.

21. Organ, C., & Kosiba, M. *A Century of Black Surgeons: The U.S. Experience* (Norman, OK: Transcript Press, 1987), 609.

Chapter 6.   Research influences and processes

1. Facio, E. "Ethnography as Personal Experience," in J. Stanfield & R. Dennis (Eds.), *Race and Ethnicity in Research Methods* (Newbury Park, CA: Sage Publications, 1993), 75-91; Fetterman, D.M. *Ethnography Step by Step* (Newbury Park,

CA: Sage Publications, 1989); Geertz, C. *The Interpretation of Cultures* (New York: Basic Books, 1973); Golden, P. (Ed.), *The Research Experience* (Itasca, IL: F.E. Peacock Publishers, 1976); Hammersley, M. *What's Wrong with Ethnography?* (New York: Routledge, 1992); Maxwell, J. *Qualitative Research Design* (Thousand Oaks, CA: Sage Publications, 1996); Strauss, A., & Corbin, J. *Basics of Qualitative Research: Grounded Theory Procedures and Techniques* (Newbury Park, CA: Sage Publications,1990).

2. Denzin, N., & Lincoln, Y. (Eds.), *Handbook of Qualitative Research* (Thousand Oaks, CA: Sage Publications, 1994), 248, 370.

3. Facio, E. "Ethnography as Personal Experience," in J. Stanfield & R. Dennis (Eds.), *Race and Ethnicity in Research Methods* (Newbury Park, CA: Sage Publications, 1993), 75-91; Stanfield, J. "Epistemological Considerations," in J. Stanfield & R. Dennis (Eds.), *Race and Ethnicity in Research Methods* (Newbury Park, CA: Sage Publications, 1993), 16-36.

4. Thomas, J. *Doing Critical Ethnography* (Newbury Park, CA: Sage Publications, 1992), 61.

5. Eichler, M. *Nonsexist Research Methods: A Practical Guide* (New York: Routledge, 1991); Fonow, M., & Cook, J. (Eds.), *Beyond Methodology: Feminist Scholarship as Lived Research* (Indianapolis, IN: Indiana University Press, 1991); Olesen, V. "Feminism and Models of Qualitative Research," in N. Denzin & Y. Lincoln (Eds.), *Handbook of Qualitative Research* (Thousand Oaks, CA: Sage Publications, 1994), 158-174; Reid, P. "Poor Women in Psychological Research," *Psychology of Women Quarterly* 17 (1993): 133-150; Roberts, H. (Ed.), *Doing Feminist Research* (New York: Routledge, 1981); Stanley, L., & Wise, S. *Breaking Out Again: Feminist Ontology and Epistemology,* second edition (New York: Routledge, 1993); Wilkinson, S. (Ed.), *Feminist Social Psychology: Developing Theory and Practice* (Philadelphia: Open University Press, 1986); Denmark, F., Russo, N., Frieze, I., & Sechzer, J. "Guidelines for Avoiding

Sexism in Psychological Research," *American Psychologist* 43 (1988): 582-585.

6. hooks, b. *Feminist Theory from Margin to Center* (Boston, MA: South End Press, 1984), 3.

7. hooks, b. *Teaching to Transgress* (New York: Routledge, 1994), 59, 61, 63, 70, 75.

8. Collins, P. Learning from the Outsider Within: The Sociological Significance of Black Feminist Thought," in M.M. Fonow & J.A. Cook (Eds.), *Beyond Methodology: Feminist Scholarship as Lived Research* (Indianapolis: Indiana University Press, 1991), 35-59.

9. Riger, S. "Epistemological Debates, Feminist Voices," *American Psychologist* 47 (1992): 730-740.

10. Olesen, V. "Feminism and Models of Qualitative Research," in N. Denzin & Y. Lincoln (Eds.), *Handbook of Qualitative Research* (Thousand Oaks, CA: Sage Publications, 1994), 158-174; Reid, P. "Poor Women in Psychological Research," *Psychology of Women Quarterly* 17 (1993): 133-150.

11. Moustakas, C. *Heuristic Research: Design, Methodology, and Applications* (Newbury Park, CA: Sage Publications, 1990), 20-21, 23-25, 27-33, 48, 52-53.

12. Bell, J. "Traumatic Event Debriefing: Service Delivery Designs and the Role of Social Work," *Social Work* 40 (1995): 36-43; Braverman, M. "Posttraumatic Crisis Intervention in the Workplace," in J. Quick, L. Murphy & J. Hurrell (Eds.), *Stress & Well-Being at Work* (APA Press, 1992), 229-316; Friedman, R., Framer, M., & Shearer, D. "Early Response to Posttraumatic Stress," *EAP Digest* (1988, Sept./Oct.): 79-83; Mitchell, J. "Stress: The History, Status and Future of Critical Incident Stress Debriefings," *JEMS* (1988, Nov.): 47-52; Spitzer, W., & Burke, L. "Practice Forum: A Critical-Incident Stress Debriefing Program for Hospital-Based Health Care Personnel," *Health & Social Work* 18 (1993): 149-156.

Chapter 7. Conclusions

1. Bell, J. "Traumatic Event Debriefing: Service Delivery Designs and the Role of Social Work," *Social Work* 40 (1995): 36-43; Braverman, M. "Posttraumatic Crisis Intervention in the Workplace," in J. Quick, L. Murphy & J. Hurrell (Eds.), *Stress & Well-Being at Work* (APA Press, 1992), 229-316; Friedman, R., Framer, M., & Shearer, D. "Early Response to Posttraumatic Stress," *EAP Digest* (1988, Sept./Oct.): 79-83; Mitchell, J. "Stress: The History, Status and Future of Critical Incident Stress Debriefings," *JEMS* (1988, Nov.): 47-52; Spitzer, W., & Burke, L. "Practice Forum: A Critical-Incident Stress Debriefing Program for Hospital-Based Health Care Personnel," *Health & Social Work* 18 (1993): 149-156.

2. hooks, b. *Sisters of the Yam: Black Women and Self-Recovery* (Boston, MA: South End Press, 1993), 152, 189.

References

Addison, R. (1984). Surviving the residency: A grounded interpretive investigation of physician socialization. Unpublished
doctoral dissertation. University of California, Berkeley.
(Order No. DA84-26889) *(Dissertation Abstracts International,* 1984, *45,* 3111)

Allen, W. (1988). Family roles, occupational statuses, and
achievement orientations among Black women in the United
States. In M.E. Malson, E. Mudimbe-Boyi, J.F. O'Barr & M.
Wyer (Eds.). *Black women in America* (pp. 79-95). Chicago:
University of Chicago Press.

Anonymous. (1983). The goal. *JAMA, 250,* 407.

Anonymous. (1994). Does anybody hear? *JAMWA, 49,* 92-93.

Aronson, E., & Mills, J. (1959). Effect of severity of initiation
on liking for a group. *Journal of Abnormal and Social
Psychology, 59,* 177-181.

Baldwin, D., Daugherty, S., & Rowley, B. (1994). Racial and
ethnic discrimination during residency: Results of a national
survey. *Acad Med, 69,* S19-21.

Bannerji, H. (1995). *Thinking through: Essays on feminism,
Marxism, and anti-racism.* Toronto, Canada: Women's Press.

Batt, R. (1972). Creating a professional identity. *American J.
Psychoanalysis, 32,* 156-162.

Becker, H., Geer, B., Hughes, E., & Strauss, A. (1961). *Boys
in white: Student culture in medical school.* Chicago:
The University of Chicago Press.

Belenky, M., Clinchy, B., Goldberger, N., & Tarule, J. (1986).
Women's ways of knowing. New York: Basic Books, Inc.

Bell, J. (1995). Traumatic event debriefing: Service delivery
designs and the role of social work. *Social Work, 40,* 36-43.

Bell-Scott, P. (Ed.) (1994). *Life notes: Personal writings by
contemporary Black women.* New York: W.W. Norton
& Company.

Bickel, J. (1988). Women in medical education: A status report. *New England Journal of Medicine, 319,* 1579-1584.

Bickel, J. (1990). Women physicians: Change agents or second-class citizens? *Humane Medicine, 6,* 101-105.

Bosk, C. (1979). *Forgive and remember: Managing medical failure.* Chicago: University of Chicago Press.

Bowman, M. & Gross, M. (1986). Overview of research on women in medicine: Issues for public policymakers. *Public Health Reports, 101,* 513-521.

Boyd, J. (1993). *In the company of my sisters: Black women and self-esteem.* New York: Dutton.

Branch, W., Pels, R., Lawrence, R., & Arky, R. (1993). Becoming a doctor: Critical-incident reports from third-year medical students. *New England Journal of Medicine, 329,* 1130-1132.

Braslow, J., & Heins, M. (1981). Women in medical education: A decade of change. *New England Journal of Medicine, 304,* 1129-1135.

Braverman, M. (1992). Posttraumatic crisis intervention in the workplace. In J. Quick, L. Murphy & J. Hurrell (Eds.). *Stress & well-being at work* (pp. 299-316). APA Press.

Bromberg, P. (1993). Shadow and substance: A relational perspective on clinical process. *Psychoanalytic Psychology, 10,* 147-168.

Bromberg, P. (1994). "Speak! that I may see you." Some reflections on dissociation, reality and psychoanalytic listening. *Psychoanalytic Dialogues, 4,* 517-547.

Bromberg, P. (1996). Standing in the spaces. The multiplicity of self and the psychoanalytic relationship. *Contemporary Psychoanalysis, 32,* 509-535.

Burke, E. (1992). Women in medicine: A promising future, despite challenging past. *Minnesota Medicine, 75,* 5.

Burlew, K. (1982). The experiences of Black females in traditional and nontraditional professions. *Psychology of Women Quarterly, 6,* 312-326.

Burnley, C., & Brukett, B. (1986). Specialization: Are women in surgery different? *JAMWA, 41,* 144.

Butcher, J. (1971). *Abnormal psychology.* Belmont, CA: Brooks/ Cole Publishing Co.

Butterfield, P. (1988). The stress of residency: A review of the literature. *Archives of Internal Medicine, 148,* 1428-135.

Bynam, J. (1985). Medical school socialization and the new physician: Role, status, adjustments, personal problems, and social identity. *Psychological Reprints, 57,* 182.

Calkins, E., Willoughby, T., & Arnold, L. (1992). Women medical students' ratings of the required surgery clerkship: Implications for career choice. *JAMA, 47,* 58-60.

Campos-Outcalt, D., Rutala, P., Witzke, D., & Fulginiti, J. (1994). Performances of underrepresented-minority students at the University of Arizona College of Medicine, 1987–1991. *Acad Med, 69,* 577-82.

Capra, F. (1982). *The turning point: Science, society, and the rising culture.* New York: Bantam.

Cherniss, D. (1980). *Staff burnout.* Beverly Hills, CA: Sage Publications.

Cherniss, C. (1995). *Beyond burnout.* New York: Routledge.

Christakis, D., & Feudtner, C. (1994). Becoming a doctor [Letter to the editor]. *New England Journal of Medicine, 330,* 720.

Cohen, M., Woodward, C., & Ferrier, B. (1988). Factors influencing career development: Do men and women differ? *JAMWA, 43,* 142-154.

Collins, P. (1988). The social construction of Black feminist thought. In M.E. Malson, E. Mudimbe-Boyi, J.F. O'Barr & M. Wyer. (Eds.). *Black women in America* (pp. 297-325). Chicago: University of Chicago Press.

Collins, P. (1991). Learning from the outsider within: The sociological significance of Black feminist thought. In M.M. Fonow & J.A. Cook (Eds.). *Beyond methodology: Feminist scholarship as lived research* (pp. 35-59). Indianapolis: Indiana University Press.

Comas-Dias, L., & Greene, B. (Eds.) (1994). *Women of color: Integrating ethnic and gender identities in psychotherapy.* New York: The Guilford Press.

Conrad, P. (1988). Learning to doctor: Reflections on recent accounts of the medical school years. *Journal of Health and Social Behavior, 29*, 323-332.

Cook, D., Liutkus, J., Risdon, C., Griffith, L., Guyatt, G., & Walter, S. (1996). Residents' experiences of abuse, discrimination and sexual harassment during residency training. *Can Med Assoc J., 154*, 1657-1665.

Coombs, R. (1978). *Mastering medicine: Professional socialization in medical school.* New York: The Free Press.

Coser, R. (1972). Authority and decision-making in a hospital: A comparative analysis. In E. Freidson & J. Lorber (Eds.), *Medical men and their work* (pp. 174-184). Chicago: Aldine Atherton.

Crandall, S., Volk, R., & Leomker, V. (1993). Medical students' attitudes toward providing care for the underserved. *JAMA, 269*, 2519-2523.

Cregler, L.; Clark, L., & Jackson, E. (1994). Careers in academic medicine and clinical practice for minorities: Opportunities and barriers. *J Assoc Acad Minor Phys, 5*, 68-73.

Creswell, J. (1994). *Research design: Qualitative and quantitative approaches.* Thousand Oaks, CA: Sage Publications.

Cross, E., Katz, J., Miller, F., & Seashore, E. (1994). *The promise of diversity.* New York: Irwin Publishing.

Csikszentmihalyi, M. (1990). *Flow: The psychology of optimal experience.* New York: HarperPerennial.

Curry, C., Trew, K., Turner, I., & Hunter J. (1994). The effect of life domains on girls' possible selves. *Adolescence, 29*, 133.

Dalton, H.L. (1995). *Racial healing: Confronting the fear between Blacks and Whites.* New York: Doubleday.

DeAngelis, C. (1991). Women in medicine: Fantasies, dreams, myths, and realities. *Am J Dis Child, 145*, 49-52.

Denmark, F., Russo, N., Frieze, I., & Sechzer, J. (1988). Guidelines for avoiding sexism in psychological research. *American Psychologist, 43*, 582-585.

Denzin, N., & Lincoln, Y. (Eds.) (1994). *Handbook of qualitative research.* Thousand Oaks, CA: Sage Publications.

Diamond, E. (1983). Women in medicine: Two points of view I. The future of women physicians. *JAMA, 249,* 207-208.

Dickinson, E. (1960). No. 108. In T.H. Johnson (Ed.). *The complete poems of Emily Dickinson.* Boston: Little Brown.

Dill, B.T. (1988). The dialectics of Black womenhood. In M.E. Malson, E. Mudimbe-Boyi, J.F. O'Barr & M. Wyer (Eds.). *Black women in America* (pp. 65-77). Chicago: University of Chicago Press.

Dreyfuss, J.H. (1995, September). Although number of women surgeons grows, women still face many challenges in surgery. *General Surgery & Laparoscopy News,* 1&18-19.

Ducker, D. (1994). Research on women physicians with multiple roles: A feminist perspective. *JAMWA, 49,* 78-84.

Dufort, F., & Maheux, B. (1995). When female medical students are the majority: Do numbers really make a difference? *JAMWA, 50,* 4-6.

Eichler, M. (1991). *Nonsexist research methods: A practical guide.* New York: Routledge.

Eisenberg, C. (1983). Women as physicians. *J. Medical Education, 58,* 534-541.

Eisenberg, C. (1989). Medicine is no longer a man's profession: Or, when the men's club goes coed it's time to change the regs. *New England J of Medicine, 321,* 1542-1544.

Elliot, D., & Girard, D. (1986). Gender and the emotional impact of internship. *JAMWA, 41,* 54-56.

Epps, R.P. (1985). The Black woman physician. *J. Natl Med Assoc, 78,* 375-381.

Eskenazi, L. & Weston, J. (1995). The pregnant plastic surgical resident: Results of a survey of women plastic surgeons and plastic surgery residency directors. *Plast Reconstr Surg, 95,* 330-335.

Essed, P. (1991). *Understanding everyday racism: An interdisciplinary theory.* Newbury Park, CA: Sage Publications.

Etter-Lewis, G., & Foster, M. (Eds.) (1996). *Unrelated kin: Race and gender in women's personal narratives.* New York: Routledge.

Facio, E. (1993). Ethnography as personal experience. In J. Stanfield & R. Dennis (Eds.), *Race and ethnicity in research methods* (pp. 75-91). Newbury Park, CA: Sage Publications.

Fausto-Sterling, A. (1992). *Myths of gender: Biological theories about men and women,* second edition. New York: Basic Books.

Ferris, L., MacKinnon, S., Mizgala, C., & McNeill, I. (1996, January). Do Canadian female surgeons feel discriminated against as women? *Can Med Assoc J., 154*(1), 21-27.

Ferris, L., Walters, B., MacKinnon, S., Mizgala, C., & McNeill, I. (1995). The quality of life of practicing Canadian women surgeons: Results of the population study. *J. of Women's Health, 4,* 87-96.

Fetterman, D. M. (1989). *Ethnography step by step.* Newbury Park, CA: Sage.

Fonow, M., & Cook, J. (Eds.) (1991). *Beyond methodology: Feminist scholarship as lived research.* Indianapolis, IN: Indiana University Press.

Freidson, E. (1970). *Professional dominance: The social structure of medical care.* New York: Atherton Press.

Freidson, E. (1975). *Doctoring together: A study of professional social control.* New York: Elsevier.

Freidson, E., & Lorber, J. (1972). *Medical men and their work.* Chicago: Aldine Atherton.

Fried, F. (1974). Commentary: Women in medicine — The training years. *J. of Operational Psychiatry, 5,* 101-102.

Friedman, R., Framer, M., & Shearer, D. (1988, September/October). Early response to posttraumatic stress. *EAP Digest, Sept./Oct.,* 79-83.

Gabram, S.G., Allen, L.W., & Deckers, P.J. (1995, January). Surgical residents in the 1990s. Issues and concerns for men and women. *Arch Surg, 130*(1), 24-28.

Geer, D.A. (1993). Women in surgery. *JAMWA, 48,* 47-50.

Geertz, C. (1973). *The interpretation of cultures.* New York: Basic Books.

Gilligan, C. (1982). *In a different voice: Psychological theory and women's development.* Cambridge, MA: Harvard Univ. Press.

Glasser, R. (1973). *Ward 402*. New York: George Braziller.

Glesne, C., & Peshkin, A. (1992). *Becoming qualitative researchers: An introduction*. White Plains, NY: Longman.

Golden, P. (Ed.) (1976). *The research experience*. Itasca, IL: F.E. Peacock Publishers.

Goodwin, N. (1985, April). The Black woman physician. *NY State J of Medicine*, 145-147.

Gordin, R., Jacobsen, S., & Rimm, A. (1991). Women in surgery: A study of first-year medical students. *American College of Surgeons Bulletin, 76*, 22-30.

Granger, N., & Renner, B. (1996). Applicant pool for emergency medicine residencies [editorial; comment], *Ann Emerg Med, 27*, 363-364.

Green, G., Wilson, J., & Lindy, J. (1985). Conceptualizing post-traumatic stress disorder: A psychosocial framework. In C.R. Figley (Ed.), *Trauma and its wake* (pp. 53-69). New York: Brunner/Mazel.

Guth, C. (1994). Pregnancy and residency [letter; comment], *Plast Reconstr Surg, 93*, 889.

Hammersley, M. (1992). *What's wrong with ethnography?* New York: Routledge.

Haug, J. (1975). A review of women in surgery. *Bulletin of the American College of Surgery, 60*, 21-23.

Hare-Mustin, R., & Maracek, J. (1990). Gender and the meaning of difference: Postmodernism and psychology. In R. Hare-Mustin & J. Mareck (Eds.), *Making a difference: Psychology and the construction of gender* (pp. 22-64). New Haven, CT: Yale University Press.

Heins, M. (1983). Women in medicine: Two points of view II. Medicine and motherhood. *JAMA, 249*, 209-210.

Higginbotham, E. (1985). *Employment for professional Black women in the twentieth century*. Memphis, TN: Center for Research on Women, Memphis State University.

Higginbotham, E. (1994). Black professional women: Job ceilings and employment sectors. In M. Zinn & B. Dill (Eds.). *Women of color in U.S. society* (pp. 113-131). Philadelphia: Temple University Press.

Hirvela, E. (1993). Surgery 2001: Twilight of the Gods. *Archives of Surgery, 128,* 658-662.

Holder, T. (1996). Women in nontraditional occupations: Information-seeking during organizational entry. *Journal of Business Communication, 33,* 9-25.

Holloway, W. (1989). Gender, psychology and science. In W. Holloway, *Subjectivity and method in psychology* (pp. 109-133). Newbury Park, CA: Sage Publications.

hooks, b. (1984). *Feminist theory from margin to center.* Boston, MA: South End Press.

hooks, b. (1993). *Sisters of the yam: Black women and self-recovery.* Boston, MA: South End Press.

hooks, b. (1994). *Teaching to transgress.* New York: Routledge.

Horney, K. (1967). *Feminine psychology.* New York: W.W. Norton and Co.

Hostler, S., & Gressard, R. (1993). Perceptions of the gender fairness of the medical education environment. *JAMWA, 48,* 51-54.

——— . How to swim with sharks (1995). *Association of Women Surgeons Newsletter, 7,* 9.

Hull, G., Bell-Scott, P., & Smith, B. (Eds.) (1982). *All the women are White, all the Blacks are men, but some of us are brave: Black women's studies.* Old Westbury, NY: Feminist Press.

Inquiry and research knowledge area study guide, Version 1.2 (1991, January). Human and Organization Development Program. Santa Barbara, CA: The Fielding Institute.

Janoff-Bulman, R. (1992). *Shattered assumptions: Towards a new psychology of trauma.* New York: The Free Press.

Jonas, H., Etzel, S., & Barazansky, B. (1992). Educational programs in U.S. medical schools. *JAMA, 268,* 1083-1090.

Jonasson, O. (1993). Women as leaders in organized surgery and surgical education: Has the time come? *Archives of Surgery, 128,* 618-621.

Josselson, R. (1990). *Finding herself: Pathways to identity development in women.* San Francisco: Jossey-Bass.

Kanter, R. (1977). *Men and women of the corporation.* New York: Basic Books.

Kaschak, E. (1992). *Engendered lives: A new psychology of women's experience.* New York: Basic Books.

Kemeny, M. (1993). Jonasson, Braunwald, and Morani: Three firsts in American surgery. *Archives of Surgery, 128,* 643-646.

Kinder, B. (1985). Women and men as surgeons: Are the problems really different? *Curr Surg, 42,* 100-104.

King, D. (1988). Multiple jeopardy, multiple consciousness: The context of a Black feminist ideology. *Signs: Journal of Women in Culture and Society, 14,* 42-72.

Koch, P., Boose, L., Cohn, M., Mansfield, P., Vickary, J., & Young, E. (1991). Coping strategies of traditionally and nontraditionally employed women at home and at work. *Health Values: Health Behavior, Education & Promotion, 15,* 19-31.

Kris, K. (1985). Developmental strains of female medical students. *JAMA, 40,* 145-148.

Kuzel, A. (1992). Sampling in qualitative inquiry. In B. Crabtree & W. Miller (Eds.). *Doing qualitative research* (pp. 31-44). Newbury Park, CA: Sage Publications.

Lazarus, R., & Lazarus, B. (1994). *Passion and reason: Making sense of our emotions.* New York: Oxford University Press.

Lewis, D. (1988). The dialectics of Black womanhood. In M.E. Malson, E. Mudimbe-Boyi, J.F. O'Barr & M. Wyer (Eds.). *Black women in America* (pp. 41-63). Chicago: University of Chicago Press.

Linn, B., & Zeppa, R. (1984). Does surgery attract students who are more resistant to stress? *Ann Surg, 200(5),* 638-643.

Lorber, J. (1984). *Women physicians: Careers, status, and power.* New York: Tavistock Publications.

Lourde, A. (1984). *Sister outsider: Essays and speeches.* Freedom, CA: The Crossing Press.

MacKinnon, S., & Mizgala, C. (1994). Pregnancy and plastic surgery residency [editorial] *Plast Reconstr Surg, 94,* 186-192.

Mandelbaum-Schmid, J. (1992, February). Women and Medicine: Are some doctors less equal than others? *MD*, 73-80.

Mandelbaum-Schmid, J. (1992, March). Women and Medicine: Are women physicians changing the practice of medicine? *MD*, 69-74.

Mandelbaum-Schmid, J. (1992, May). Women and Medicine: An unequal past, a common future. *MD*, 87-98.

Maran, A., Cudworth, J., Doig, C., & Wilson, J. (1993, October). Women in surgery in Scotland: a working party of the Royal College of Surgeons of Edinburgh. *J R Coll Surg Edinb, 38*(5), 279-284.

Martin, M. (1996). Applicant pool for emergency medicine residency programs: Information on minority and female applicants. *Ann Emerg Med, 27*, 331-338.

Martin, S., Arnold, R., & Parker, R. (1988). Gender and medical socialization. *Journal of Health & Social Behavior, 29*, 333-343.

Martin, S., Parker, R., & Arnold, R. (1988). Careers of women physicians: Choices and constraints. In Women and Medicine (Special Issue). *Western Journal of Medicine, 149*, 758-760.

Maxwell, J. (1996). *Qualitative research design.* Thousand Oaks, CA: Sage Publications.

McGoldrick, M., Garcia-Preto, N., Moore Hines, P., & Lee, E. (1989). Ethnicity and women. In M. McGoldrick, C. Anderson & Walsh, F. (Eds). *Women in families* (pp. 169-199). New York: W.W. Norton & Co.

McGuire, M. (1982). The woman physician's credibility: Problems and stratagems. *JAMWA, 37*, 317-325.

McIntosh, P. (1988). *White privilege and male privilege: A personal account of coming to see correspondences through work in women's studies.* Wellesley, MA: The Stone Center at Wellesley College.

McNamara, M. (1985). Women surgeons: How much of an impact? *Curr Surg, 42*, 94-100.

Meichenbaum, D., Price, R., Phares, E.J., McCormick, N., & Hyde, J. (1989). *Exploring choices — The psychology of adjustment.* Boston, MA: Scott, Foresman and Co.

Miller, S. (1970). *Prescription for leadership: Training for the medical elite.* Chicago: Aldine Publishing.

Mitchell, J. (1988, November). Stress: The history, status and future of critical incident stress debriefings. *JEMS,* 47-52.

Mizgala, C., MacKinnon, S., Walters, B., Ferris, L., McNeill, I., & Knighton, T. (1993). Women surgeons: Results of the Canadian population study. *Annals of Surgery, 218,* 37-46.

Mizrahi, T. (1986). *Getting rid of patients: Contradictions in the socialization of physicians.* New Brunswick, NJ: Rutgers University Press.

Moraga, C., & Anzaldua, G. (Eds.) (1981). *This bridge called my back: Writings by radical women of color.* Watertown, MA: Persephone Press.

Moore, F., & Priebe, C. (1991). Board-certified physicians in the United States, 1971–1986. *New England Journal of Medicine, 324,* 536-543.

Morrison, T. (Ed.) (1992). *Race-ing justice, en-gendering power.* New York: Pantheon Books.

Moustakas, C. (1990). *Heuristic research: Design, methodology, and applications.* Newbury Park, CA: Sage Publications.

Mullings, L. (1994). Images, ideology, and women of color. In M. Zinn & B. Dill (Eds.). *Women of color in U.S. society* (pp. 265-289). Philadelphia: Temple University Press.

Mumford, E. (1970). *Interns: From students to physicians.* Cambridge, MA: Harvard University Press.

Myers, M. (1996). Abuse of residents: It's time to take action [editorial; comment]. *Can Med Assoc J., 154,* 1705-1708.

Neumayer, L., Freischlag, J., & Levinson, W. (1994). Demographics of today's woman surgeon. *American College of Surgeons Bulletin, 79,* 28-33.

Neumayer, L., Konishi, G., L'Archeveque, D., Choi, R., Ferrario, T., McGrath, J., Nakawatase, T., Freischlag, J., & Levison, W. (1993). Female surgeons in the 1990s: Academic role models. *Archives of Surgery, 128,* 669-672.

Notman, M., & Nadelson, C. (1973). Medicine: A career conflict for women. *American J. Psychiatry, 130,* 1123-1127.

O'Connell, A., & O'Connell, V. (1992). *Choice and change: The psychology of holistic growth, adjustment, and creativity.* Englewood Cliffs, NJ: Prentice Hall.

O'Leary, V., Unger, R., & Wallston, B. (Eds.) (1985). *Women, gender, and social psychology.* Hillsdale, NJ: Lawrence Erlbaum Associates, Publishers.

Olesen, V. (1994). Feminism and models of qualitative research. In N. Denzin & Y. Lincoln (Eds.). *Handbook of qualitative research* (pp. 158-174). Thousand Oaks, CA: Sage Publications.

Organ, C. (1995). Good news in the Greenvilles of America [editorial]. *Arch Surg, 130,* 1033-1034.

Organ, C., & Kosiba, M. (1987). *A century of Black surgeons: The U.S. experience.* Norman, OK: Transcript Press.

Ortiz, F. (1975). Women in medicine: The process of professional incorporation. *JAMWA, 30,* 18-30.

Osborne, D. (1983, April 3). My wife, the doctor: Have women humanized medicine? *This World,* 8-10.

Pamies R., Lawrence L., Helm E., & Strayhorn G. (1994). The effects of certain student and institutional characteristics on minority medical student specialty choice. *J Natl Med Assoc, 86,* 136-40.

Parson, E. (1985). Ethnicity and traumatic stress: The intersecting point in psychotherapy. In C.R. Figley (Ed.), *Trauma and its wake* (pp. 314-337). New York: Brunner/Mazel.

Pasterna, J. (1993). Women in surgery: An ancient tradition. *Archives of Surgery, 128,* 622-626.

Peebles, R. (1989). Female surgeons in the U.S.: An 18-year review. *American College of Surgeons Bulletin, 74,* 18-23.

Pinderhughes, E. (1989). *Understanding race, ethnicity, and power.* New York: The Free Press.

Ramos, S. & Feiner, C. (1989). Women surgeons: A national survey. *JAMWA, 44,* 21-25.

Reid, P. (1993). Poor women in psychological research. *Psychology of Women Quarterly, 17,* 133-150.

Reid, P., & Kelly, E. (1994). Research on women of color: From ignorance to awareness. *Psychology of Women Quarterly, 18,* 477-486.

Relman, A. (1980). Here come the women. *N. Engl. J Med, 302,* 1252-1253.

Rich, A. (1979). Toward a woman-centered university. In A. Rich, *On lies, secrets, and silence* (pp. 125-155). New York: W.W. Norton & Co.

Richmond-Abbott, M. (1992). *Masculine & feminine: Gender roles over the life cycle,* second edition. New York: McGraw-Hill, Inc.

Riger, S. (1992). Epistemological debates, feminist voices. *American Psychologist, 47,* 730-740.

Roberts, H. (Ed.) (1981). *Doing feminist research.* New York: Routledge.

Rothman, R. (1993). *Inequality and stratification: Class, color, and gender.* Englewood Cliffs, NJ: Prentice Hall.

Sandrick, K. (1992). The residency experience: The woman's perspective. *American College of Surgeons Bulletin, 77,* 10-17.

Scales, A. (1990). Surviving legal de-education: An outsider's guide. *Vermont Law Review, 15,* 139-163.

Schneider, S., & Phillips, W. (1993). Depression and anxiety in medical, surgical, and pediatric interns. *Psychol Rep, 72,* 1145-1146.

Scheuneman, A., Pickleman, J., & Freeark, R. (1985). Age, gender, lateral dominance in prediction of operative skill among several residents. *Surgery, 98,* 506-514.

Schwartz, R., Barclay, J., Harrell, P., Murphy, A., Jarecky, R., & Donnelly, M. (1994). Defining the surgical personality: A preliminary study. *Surgery, 115,* 62-68.

Scrignar, C. (1988). *Post-traumatic stress disorder,* second edition. New Orleans, LA: Bruno Press.

Sheldon, G. (May, 1993). Recruitment and selection of the best and brightest. *Ann Thoracic Surgery, 55*(5), 1340-1344.

Shem, S. (1978). *The house of God.* New York: Marek.

Sherman, S., & Rosenblatt, A. (1984). Women physicians as teachers, administrators, and researchers in medical and surgical specialties: Kanter versus "Avis" as competing hypotheses. *Sex Roles, 11,* 203-209.

Shuval, J. (1975). From "boy" to "colleague": Processes of role transformation in professional socialization. *Social Science & Medicine, 9,* 413-420.

Spitzer, W., & Burke, L. (1993). Practice forum: A critical-incident stress debriefing program for hospital-based health care personnel. *Health & Social Work, 18,* 149-156.

Stack, C. (1984). Different voices, different visions: Gender, culture, and moral reasoning. In M. Zinn & B. Dill (Eds.). *Women of color in U.S. society* (pp. 291-314). Philadelphia: Temple University Press.

Stake, R. (1994). Case Studies. In N.K. Denzin & Y.S. Lincoln (Eds.), *Handbook of qualitative research* (pp. 236-247). Thousand Oaks, CA: Sage Publications.

Stanfield, J. (1993). Epistemological considerations. In J. Stanfield & R. Dennis (Eds.). *Race and ethnicity in research methods* (pp. 16-36). Newbury Park, CA: Sage Publications.

Stanley, L., & Wise, S. (1993). *Breaking out again: Feminist ontology and epistemology,* second edition. New York: Routledge.

Sterling, R. (1987). Female surgeons: The dawn of a new era. In C.H. Organ & M. Kosiba (Eds.). *A century of Black surgeons* (pp. 581-610). Norman, OK: Transcript Press.

Strauss, A., & Corbin, J. (1990). *Basics of qualitative research: Grounded theory procedures and techniques.* Newbury Park, CA: Sage Publications.

Strayhorn, G. (1980). Perceived stress and social support of Black and White medical students. *J. Med. Educ., 55,* 618-620.

Strayhorn, G. (1996). Underrepresentation in the applicant pool for emergency medicine residencies [editorial; comment]. *Ann Emerg Med, 27,* 364-366.

Sue, D.W., & Sue, D. (1990). *Counseling the culturally different.* New York: John Wiley & Sons.

Tardiff, K., Cella, D., Seiferth, C., & Perry, S. (1986). Selection and change of specialties by medical school graduates. *J Med Educ, 31,* 790.

Thomas, J. (1993). *Doing critical ethnography.* Newbury Park, CA: Sage Publications.

Trickett, E., Watts, R., & Birman, D. (Eds.) (1994). *Human diversity.* San Francisco: Jossey-Bass Publishers.

U.S. Department of Health, Education, and Welfare, Public Health Service, Health Resources Administration Bureau of Health Manpower (1978). *Study of physician socialization* (HRP-0901269). Springfield, VA: National Technical Information Service.

U.S. Department of Health and Human Services, Public Health Service, Council on Graduate Medical Education (1995). *Fifth report: Women & medicine* (HRSA-P-DM-95-1). Washington, DC: U.S. Government Printing Office.

Ulstad, V. (1993). How women are changing medicine. *JAMWA, 48,* 75-78.

Walters, B. (1993). Why don't more women choose surgery as a career? *Acad Med, 68,* 350-351.

Wear, D. (Ed.) (1996). *Women in medical education: An anthology of experience.* Albany, NY: State University of New York Press.

Webb, C., Herbert, J., & Waugh, F. (1993). Predictors of Black students' board performances: MCAT scores are not the whole story [letter]. *Acad Med, 68,* 204-205.

Webb, C., Waugh, F., & Herbert, J. (1993). Relationship between locus of control and performance on the National Board of Medical Examiners, Part I, among black medical students. *Psychol Rep, 72,* 1171-1177.

Weston, J. (1993, March). Winds of change [editorial]. *Ann Plastic Surg, 30*(3), 287-288.

White, J. (1984). *The psychology of Blacks: An Afro-American perspective.* Englewood Cliffs, NJ: Prentice Hall.

Wilkinson, S. (Ed.) (1986). *Feminist social psychology: Developing theory and practice.* Philadelphia: Open University Press.

Williams, A., Domnick-Pierre, K., Vayda, E., Stevenson, H., & Burke, M. (1990). Women in medicine: Practice patterns and attitudes. *Canadian Medical Assoc. J., 143,* 194-201.

Wilson, J., Smith, W.K., & Johnson, S. (1985). A comparative analysis of PTSD among various survivor groups. In C.R. Figley (Ed.). *Trauma and its wake* (pp. 142-172). New York: Brunner/Mazel.

Wolman, C., & Frank, H. (1975). The solo woman in a professional peer group. *American J. Orthopsychiatry, 45,* 164-171.

Wray, R. (1993). Pregnancy and plastic surgery residency [editorial]. *Plast Reconstr Surg, 91,* 344-345.

Wright, L. (1589). *Display of Dutie.*

Yogev, S., & Harris, S. (1983). Women physicians during residency years: Workload, work satisfaction and self-concept. *Soc. Sci. Med., 17,* 837-841.

Young-Eisendrath, P. (1996). *The resilient spirit: Transforming suffering into insight and renewal.* New York: Addison-Wesley Publishing Co, Inc.

Young-Shumate, L., Kramer, T., & Beresin, E. (1993). Pregnancy during graduate medical training. *Acad Med, 86,* 792-799.

Zeldow, P., & Daugherty, S. (1991). Personality profiles and specialty choices of students from two medical school classes. *Acad Med, 66,* 283.

APPENDIX A

Introductory Letter

(Letterhead)

Date

XXXXXXXX
XXXXXXXX
XXXXXXXX

Dear Dr. XXXXXX;

You have been identified as a practicing Black female general surgeon. I am a practicing Black female general surgeon and a doctoral student at The Fielding Institute in Santa Barbara, CA. My dissertation research is on the residency experience of Black women general surgeons. I am inviting you to participate with me in this research.

This research has two parts. I am hoping to identify all of the practicing Black female general surgeons in the U.S. Each woman is being sent the enclosed brief survey. For the second part, a smaller number of women — six to ten — will be invited to participate in an in-depth interview with me to discuss their residency experience. This interview will take about two hours and will be scheduled at a time and site convenient to the participant. Interviewees will also be given the opportunity to attend a discussion of the findings of this research, to be scheduled in conjunction with a national surgical meeting. All information will be kept confidential, unless expressly agreed to by the participant. All data will be reported in either aggregate fashion or anonymously, unless expressly agreed to by the participant. Please see the enclosed informed consent forms.

I hope that you will choose to participate in this research. I think that it will be a remarkable experience for all involved. Please complete the enclosed informed consent form and survey instrument and return to me in the enclosed envelope ASAP. The survey should take you about 15 minutes to complete. If you have any questions, please contact me. Thank you very much for your assistance.

Sincerely yours,

Patricia L. Dawson, MD, FACS

APPENDIX B

Survey of Black Female General Surgeons

Name _____

Address _____

_____

_____

Phone/Day _____ P.M. _____

Fax _____

E-mail _____

Date of birth _____

Father's occupation _____

Father's highest level of education _____

Mother's occupation _____

Mother's highest level of education _____

Undergraduate school attended _____

Medical school attended _____

Year of graduation from medical school_____

Surgical residency program(s) _____

_____

_____

Year of residency completion _____

Fellowship program(s)_____

_____

_____

Year of fellowship completion _____

Sub-specialty certification: _____

Type _____

Date _____

Practice areas of special interest _____

_____

Board certified   Yes _____   No _____   Year _____
Board eligible   Yes _____   No _____
ACS Fellow   Yes _____   No _____   Year _____

What influenced your choice of general surgery as a career?

_____

_____

Would you be willing to participate in an interview with me on your residency experience? Each interview will last about two hours and will be scheduled at site and time convenient to you.

Yes _____ No _____

Would you be interested in attending a discussion of the findings of this research to be scheduled in conjunction with a national surgical meeting? The discussion would last about two hours and be open to all interested Black women surgeons.

Yes _____ No _____

Other researchers may contact me for names and addresses of women participating in my research. Are you willing to have your name and address given to other researchers?

Yes _____ No _____

(None of the data you provide in this research will
be given out without your express permission.)

I want to send this survey to all practicing Black female general surgeons in the U.S. Please provide me with the names, addresses and telephone numbers of any other practicing Black female general surgeons that you know (use another page if necessary).

_____

_____

_____

THANK YOU FOR YOUR PARTICIPATION!

Please return to me by _____

APPENDIX C

Informed Consent Form
Survey of Black Female General Surgeons

═══════════════════════════════════════

I agree to participate in the research study conducted by Patricia L. Dawson, MD, a doctoral student in the Human and Organization Development Program at The Fielding Institute, Santa Barbara, CA. I understand that the research involves collecting data about practicing Black female general surgeons and their residency experiences. I have been selected for this study because I am a practicing Black female general surgeon.

I understand that the study has two parts: a survey questionnaire and a face-to-face interview. I understand that this consent is for the first part of the study and that participation will require that I complete a brief questionnaire about myself, my medical education and surgical training. This survey will take approximately 15 minutes to complete. Survey data will be reported in aggregate fashion only.

I may also be asked to participate in a personal interview lasting approximately two hours. Interview participants will be mailed transcripts of their interview and the Researcher's tentative findings and interpretations. I will be asked to verify and comment on the materials. These activities should take approximately one hour to complete. I understand that I will be briefed further by the Researcher if I am asked to participate in the second phase of this study. Total time commitment for both the survey completion and interview participation should not exceed four hours.

I understand that the information that I provide will be kept strictly confidential, except with my express permission. The survey instruments will be reviewed only by individuals involved with this research project. The interview tape recordings will be listened to only by individuals involved with this research project. I will be asked to provide a different name for any quotes that might be included in the final research report. I will also have the opportunity to remove any quotations when I review the transcripts. In addition, the surveys, tapes and all related research materials will be kept in a secure file cabinet and destroyed five years after the completion of this study. The results of this research will be described as part of Patricia Dawson's doctoral dissertation and may be reported in other forums — journal articles, books, presentations, workshops, etc. The Fielding Institute Research Ethics Committee has approved this research and has access to any and all materials related to this research project.

I understand that I may develop a greater personal awareness of my residency experience as a result of my participation in this research. Other benefits to me may include an opportunity to reflect on my personal experiences; an opportunity to be seen and heard in a possibly new way: "debriefing" of a possibly stressful experience; introduction to a cohort of similar others; and an opportunity to collaborate in the creation of knowledge. I understand that participating in this study could involve bringing to my awareness painful memories and emotions. Should I experience discomfort related to this, I understand that the Researcher is available to me at the phone number listed below to discuss my reactions. In addition, I may withdraw from this study at any time (either during or after the interview) without negative consequences. Should I withdraw, my data will be eliminated from the study and will be destroyed.

I understand that I will not receive any financial compensation for my participation in this research.

In addition to having an opportunity to review and comment on the study materials, I know that I may request a copy of the summary findings of this study by completing and returning the attached form. I also realize that I may contact the Researcher to ask any questions about the study at any time.

I have read and understood the above and I agree to participate in the *survey* phase of this study. I will sign one copy of this informed consent form and return it to the Researcher. I will keep the second copy for my own reference.

_____

NAME OF PARTICIPANT (please print)

_____

SIGNATURE OF PARTICIPANT

_____

DATE

Patricia L. Dawson, MD
[Contact information]

☐ If you would like a copy of the findings
of this study, please check here.

APPENDIX D

Interview Outline

Introduction and expression of appreciation for their participation.

Description of research and review of purpose.

How did you decide to become a general surgeon?

Tell me about your residency experience.

Potential prompts:

- Where did you do your training?

- Were there other women residents?
  Other Black female residents?

- What was your most enjoyable experience?

- What was your most difficult or stressful experience?

- How did your experiences compare with those of your peers?

- How did your being a Black woman influence your residency experience?

How would you characterize or describe general surgeons?
Does this description fit you?

What was the overall impact of your residency experience on you as a person and on your life?

What were you like before and after your residency?
Are you different now?

Was there anything that you needed in residency that was not available? What was it?

- Role models, mentors?
- Psychological support?
- Peer/support group?
- Family support?

Did you have supports during your residency? What were they?

- Role models, mentors?
- Psychological support?
- Peer/support group?
- Family support?

How would you change your residency experience/program?

What metaphor would you use to describe surgery?

Are there other things you would like to talk about in regard to your residency?

Is there anything else you would like to talk about before we close?

How has this interview been for you?

Thank you very much for your participation.

APPENDIX E

Informed Consent Form
Interview of Black Female General Surgeons

I agree to participate in the research study conducted by Patricia L. Dawson, MD, a doctoral student in the Human and Organization Development Program at The Fielding Institute, Santa Barbara, CA. I understand that the research involves collecting data about practicing Black female general surgeons and their residency experiences. I have been selected for this study because I am a practicing Black female general surgeon.

I understand that the study has two parts: a survey questionnaire and a face-to-face interview. I understand that this consent is for the interview phase of the study.

I have been asked to participate in a personal interview lasting approximately two hours. The topic of the interview will be my residency experiences. Interview participants will be mailed transcripts of their interview and the Researcher's tentative findings and interpretations. I will be asked to verify and comment on the materials. These activities should take approximately one hour to complete. I have already completed the survey portion of this study. Total time commitment for both the survey completion and interview participation should not exceed four hours.

I understand that the information that I provide will be kept strictly confidential, except with my express permission. The survey instruments will be reviewed only by individuals involved in this research project. The tape recordings will be listened to only by individuals involved in this research project. I give permission to use quotes and I will provide a different name for any quotes that might be included in the final research report. I will also have the opportunity to remove any quotations when I review the transcripts. In addition, the surveys, tapes and all related research materials will be kept in a secure file cabinet and destroyed five years after the completion of this study. The results of this research will be described as part of Patricia Dawson's doctoral dissertation and may be reported in other forums — journal articles, books, presentations, workshops, etc. The Fielding Institute Research Ethics Committee has approved this research and has access to any and all materials related to this research project.

I understand that I may develop a greater personal awareness of my residency experience as a result of my participation in this research. Other benefits to me may include an opportunity to reflect on my personal experiences; an opportunity to be seen and heard in a possibly new way: "debriefing" of a possibly stressful experience; introduction to a cohort of similar others; and an opportunity to collaborate in the creation of knowledge. I understand that participating in this study could involve bringing to my awareness painful memories and emotions. Should I experience discomfort related to this, I understand that the Researcher is available to me at the phone number listed below to discuss my reactions. In addition, I may withdraw from this study at any time (either during or after the interview) without negative consequences. Should I withdraw my data will be eliminated from the study and will be destroyed.

I understand that I will not receive any financial compensation for my participation in this research.

In addition to having an opportunity to review and comment on the study materials, I know that I may request a copy of the summary findings of this study by completing and returning the attached form. I also realize that I may contact the Researcher to ask any questions about the study at any time.

I have read and understood the above and I agree to participate in the *interview* phase of this study. I will sign one copy of this informed consent form and return it to the Researcher. I will keep the second copy for my own reference.

For the reporting of the study data I would like to use a pseudonym:

_____
PSEUDONYM

_____
NAME OF PARTICIPANT (please print)

_____
SIGNATURE OF PARTICIPANT

_____
DATE

Patricia L. Dawson, MD
[Contact information]

☐ If you would like a copy of the findings
of this study, please check here.

APPENDIX F

Survey Results: Fathers' Occupations

Aeronautical engineer
Airplane mechanic (2)
Auto mechanic
Biochemist
Biochemistry professor
Businessman
Electrician
Financial planner
Machinist
Mailman
Mechanical engineer
Minister
Musician
Pharmacist
Physician (3)
Policeman
Quality control inspector
Sales executive
Surgeon (2)
Taxi driver

APPENDIX G

Survey Results: Mothers' Occupations

Administrative assistant
Civil servant
Homemaker (6)
Housekeeper
Lab tech
Law student
LPN
Medical administrator
Nurse's aide
Pharmacist
Research assistant
RN (2)
RN practitioner
Salesperson
School principal
Secretary (2)
Teacher (4)

APPENDIX H

Survey Results: Undergraduate Schools

Allegheny College
Andrews University
Boston University
Bryn Mawr College
Cornell University
George Washington University
Harvard University
Hofstra University
Howard University (2)
Johns Hopkins University (2)
Lafayette College
Long Island University
Marymount College
Princeton University
San Jose State University
Spelman College
Swarthmore College
Tuskegee University
University of California, Berkeley
University of Miami
University of Rochester
Virginia Commonwealth University
Wesleyan University
Yale University

APPENDIX I

Survey Results: Medical Schools

Case Western Reserve University (2)
Columbia University of Physicians and Surgeons (2)
Drew University at University of California, Los Angeles
Georgetown University
Harvard University
Howard University (3)
Jefferson Medical College
Johns Hopkins University
Loma Linda University
Medical College of Virginia (2)
Morehouse School of Medicine
New Jersey Medical School —
    University of Medicine and Dentistry of NJ
State University of New York Health Science Center
State University of New York, Syracuse
Tufts University
University of Illinois
University of Miami
Washington University School of Medicine
Yale University

APPENDIX J

Survey Results: Residency

Alton Ochsner Medical Foundation
Duke
George Washington
Harbor University of California, Los Angeles
Harlem Hospital
Howard (5)
Kaiser Oakland
King Drew Medical Center
Loma Linda Medical Center
Medical College of Virginia
Montefiore
New Jersey Medical School —
    University of Medicine and Dentistry of NJ (3)
New York Medical College
Oregon Health Sciences University
St. Agnes, Baltimore
St. Joseph Mercy Hospital
St. Luke's — Roosevelt, NY
St. Vincent's Medical Center, Connecticut
State University of New York, Buffalo
The New York Hospital, Cornell Medical Center
University of California, San Francisco
University of Chicago
University of Illinois
University of Minnesota
University of Southern California
University of Washington
Vanderbilt University
Virginia Mason Medical Center

APPENDIX K

Survey Results: Influences

Role model in medical school
Ability to help people by operating
Pathophysiology of disease
Working with hands / technical aspects (5)
Being able to "fix" problems (3)
Continuity of care
Immediate gratification (3)
Variety of challenges (3)
Enjoyed surgery most (4)
The pace
Control of work environment
Fun
Suits my temperament
Defined hierarchy
Medical school experiences (4)
Father
Experience as EMT
Surgeons' approach to problems
Operating room environment
Family members
So few Black women in surgery
Always wanted to be surgeon
The book *The Making of a Woman Surgeon,*
    Elizabeth Morgan, 1980. NY: Putnam
Active, comprehensive participation in patients' care (2)

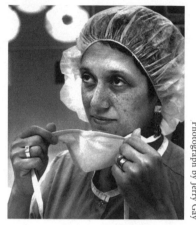

Photograph by Jerry Gay

PATRICIA L. DAWSON, M.D., Ph.D., FACS, a breast surgeon in private practice in Seattle, Washington, earned her medical degree from New Jersey Medical School in Newark. She completed two years of general surgical residency training at the University of Medicine and Dentistry in Newark and three years at Virginia Mason Medical Center in Seattle. She practiced general surgery for one year in private practice and for fourteen years at Group Health Cooperative of Puget Sound, Seattle; she then returned to private practice.

It was during her tenure as director of medical staff diversity for Group Health Cooperative that Dr. Dawson began her first investigations into the negative aspects of surgical residency training as experienced by Black female surgeons. Pursuing this topic further, she earned a Ph.D. in Human and Organizational Systems from the Fielding Institute in Santa Barbara, California.

Dr. Dawson lives in Seattle with her husband, Stanley Hiserman, their children, Alexandria and Wesley, her mother, E. Claire Dawson, and three very entertaining cats.

COLOPHON

The body of this book was typeset in 11-point Adobe Sabon Roman, a descendant of the Garamond and Granjon type families. Sabon, designed by Jan Tschichold in 1964, is a registered trademark of Linotype–Hell AG and/or its subsidiaries.